THIS TOO SHALL PASS

THIS TOO SHALL PASS

Encouragement for Parents Who Sometimes Doubt Their Teens Were Created in the Image of God

Kel Groseclose

DIMENSIONS
FOR LIVING

NASHVILLE

THIS TOO SHALL PASS

Library of Congress Cataloging-in-Publication Data

Groseclose, Kel, 1940–
    This too shall pass : encouragement for parents who sometimes doubt their teens were created in the image of God / Kel Groseclose.
        p. cm.
    ISBN 0-687-00610-4 (pbk. : alk. paper)
    1. Parents—Religious life. 2. Parenting—Religious aspects—Christianity. 3. Parent and teenager. I. Title.
BV4845.G74   1995
248.8'45—dc20   95–20230
                                                                                    CIP

95 96 97 98 99 00 01 02 03 04 — 10 9 8 7 6 5 4 3 2 1

MANUFACTURED IN THE UNITED STATES OF AMERICA

TO

Corey, Tyler, Ashley, and Haley, special grand-
children all. In the teen years, I do not ask for an
easy time for you and your parents but rather for
strength and courage. May you grow by leaps
and bounds in those seven years. And may your
dear parents see a dim light not only at the end of
the tunnel, but a bright and beautiful glow in the
tunnel as well.

CONTENTS

Contents

1.
This Too Shall Pass

What do you say to a group of farmers in the Midwest, people who love the land and their livestock but who probably haven't had a vacation in years; dear folk who are in debt up to their ears; who are literally married to their work, committed to it day after day from before the sun rises to long after it sets, for richer but mostly for poorer? In an address to the Wisconsin Agricultural Society in 1849, Abraham Lincoln spun a yarn. He told a story of a Middle Eastern monarch who called together the wise persons of the realm. "Invent me a sentence," he charged them, "that will always and everywhere be true."

After much debate, they returned with these words: "And this, too, shall pass away." Lincoln reflected on how profound this simple phrase is, remarking that it both humbles the proud and consoles the afflicted. I would venture to guess that along with farmers, parents of teenagers have uttered these words countless times, often accompanied by a sigh and a shrug of their shoulders.

Parenting young people has several similarities to farming. In both tasks the hours are long and the pay small, yet you willingly and gladly make sacrifices. You do your best while praying without ceasing. You sit and hope and trust because the harvest is not up to you. It's in God's hands. You plant the seeds, water, nourish, protect, and give tender care. Then all that remains is to wait and watch, as patiently as possible, to see what the final results will be.

It is actually no crime to be thirteen, to start the journey through the teen years. We have all been there and have somehow managed to survive. The problem with our son was that he stayed thirteen. Sure he had birthdays. But what does arithmetic know about raising teenagers? According to our calculations, he was thirteen for five full years, very long and exceedingly full years. He was eighteen before his brain and emotions finally caught up with his hormones. Then his transformation to a responsible, reasonable young man took place quickly. He seemed to mature five years in five days. It was amazing and of no small relief to his weary parents.

In retrospect, I'm certain he didn't intend to be that way. He just couldn't help it. He pushed and tested even the tiniest limits we set. He perfected the art of pouting. He could grump and mope with the best of them. He told us as parents we were stupid and old-fashioned in a thousand creative but equally frustrating and painful ways. Sometimes we didn't understand his choice of words but we knew THAT look and tone of voice. I suppose we could have tried harder to see the bright side. Even fifteen years later, however, the only positive thing I can find is that it may have improved his verbal skills as much as eighth grade English did.

The phrase "This too shall pass" may always and forever be true. It fails, though, to include a timetable. It neglects to say when "this" will be over and done with. Being the parent of a teen does have an ending date, exactly seven years after its beginning. But crammed into those years can be several centuries, a millennium or two, and occasionally an eternity. As a parent who now looks back upon these years, let me assure you from my perspective that they went by all too quickly. It's hard to believe that our youngest is now twenty. I do confess I remember days that seemed endless, and I watched out the front window for nights that lasted forever. The years will fly by. I guarantee it. It's those pesky little days that will cause bags under your eyes and your fingernails to be chewed to the quick.

This phrase is not an excuse for do-nothing, thumb-twiddling, passive parenting. The awareness that a teen's tumult and turmoil will last a limited length of time does not give parents license to take a seven-year sabbatical; to totally ignore her, to stop communicating, caring, and disciplining him until the supposedly magic age of twenty finally arrives.

We might call this an Advanced Course in Planned Parenthood. If a great deal of preparation, intentionality, and thought go into making the original decision to bring a life into the world, shouldn't that same commitment continue all the way along? To nurture a life toward growth and maturity is not a task for the fainthearted. Sometimes keeping silence requires greater strength than speaking out. Waiting is hard work. Believe me, as a parent of six I know what I'm talking about.

I have total recall of what it was like when each of ours turned sixteen and got their driver's licenses. Those first solo excursions in the car were probably worse for us as parents than for them as inexperienced drivers, although their stories of driving our old family station wagon, the huge gray boat with half the paint peeled off, indicates it may have been a draw. Our parental concern and their embarrassment probably canceled each other out. Even though they almost always honored our mutually established curfews, we still worried. We tried to remain calm. Mom and I gave each other frequent pep talks and other reassurances. But we both lay in bed with our eyes shut, pretending to be resting, while our ears listened to every tiny noise outside, our brains on full-scale alert. When we finally heard the car turn into the driveway and the front door of the house click shut, then and only then did we completely relax, kiss each other goodnight, and doze off.

Parents of teens should probably read everything on the subject they can get their hands on, then mix and match the different theories to fit their particular situation. There is no one right way to raise children of any age. Look for general principles and common threads of wisdom. Accept most of the advice you receive, unsolicited or otherwise, not only with a grain of salt but with an entire saltshaker handy.

While families share characteristics, each one on the face of this earth has unique qualities as well. Just when you think you've got your young person or persons figured out, they're sure to make a U-turn, a 180-degree change of direction. Their intention is not to make parents feel dumb or incompetent, although it usually does. It's that they're growing so rapidly that the old patterns of behavior simply aren't adequate. Parents of teens had better be able to accept constant and rapid change. Supple, limber personalities are necessary ingredients for all parents, especially those with teens under their roofs.

It's also quite helpful to learn to delight in small and temporary pleasures. Discover the joys of modest successes and tiny accomplishments. Take it a day at a time. Parenting teens is not simply a matter of gritting your teeth and surviving to the bitter end. It can be a great and marvelous adventure together. There'll be detours and dead ends, lots of them. But parents should consider it a high honor, a significant privilege to be entrusted to walk with young persons for those seven special years.

Teens have the amazing capacity both to give you energy and to take it away, to build you up and wear you out, and to keep you guessing which it will be at any given moment. At a school concert, game, or awards assembly, you may nearly burst with pride. Barely two minutes after it's over, you may be so aggravated you're sputtering and fuming. Same kid. Same parent. Just another verse to an old song of being a family.

When you and I are down in those parental trenches slogging along, it's pretty difficult to see the possibilities of the future. All we tend to notice are the problems of the present. That's when we need to repeat over and over, "This too shall pass." It will. Understanding the temporary nature of the teenage years helps us maintain a healthy perspective of the job. If you know it's not going to last forever, it's far easier to be patient, to keep a sense of humor, to put up with five-course meals noisily prepared at midnight, to handle inconveniences like never having cash in your wallet or purse, and to listen to loud music you wouldn't appreciate even at *pianissimo*.

There really aren't any simple answers to successfully helping teenagers mature into solid, productive, well-adjusted adults. An expert in this field is almost certainly an individual who either has not yet lived with one, or who parented one so many years ago he or she has conveniently forgotten everything but the happy times. We can talk about principles and guidelines and trends. But the keys to successful parenting are unconditional love and a genuine caring for persons from the ages of thirteen to nineteen. Knowing the theories and techniques of parenting is indeed helpful, yet there is no substitute for total commitment to the task.

By the time children reach the teen years, parents have taken and hopefully passed a variety of other parenting tests. They've discovered ways through other obstacles, met many challenges, and built a certain amount of confidence in their abilities to make wise decisions, maintain composure, and provide effective discipline. Parents may well need every bit of that previous twelve years' experience to sustain them through the next seven.

The fact that you bought this book may indicate that you have a fast-growing, constantly hungry, bathroom-camping teen on the premises; one who is no longer that sweet, trusting, innocent child of but a few months ago. That young person who so recently looked up to you with admiration now literally looks down on you with a confusing mixture of impatience and appreciation, of embarrassment and love. You cannot accurately predict which emotional response they will make in any given situation. That is because your teen probably doesn't know, either. It is therefore the parents' role to be capable of adjusting to whatever feelings are directed their way, accepting their youth "for better or for worse."

The awareness that "This too shall pass" provides parents with an advantage, slight though it may be, in dealing with teenagers.

You can outlast them. You're not any smarter. In fact, when it comes to computers, electronic gadgets, learning a second language, doing algebraic word problems, playing a musical instrument, and participating in athletic endeavors, parents may well be at a significant disadvantage. What parents do have going for them is persistence, bordering sometimes on stubbornness. They have a historical perspective that their offspring cannot have yet gained. Age and experience do have their benefits, and parents ought to draw on them as often as possible.

Yes, there will be nights when you toss and turn, when you awaken in the morning wearier than when you went to bed. You will frequently find yourself at your wit's end. Adult wits are finite with definite limits, a truth that most teens instinctively know. When they sense you are close to the border, the more likely they are to try finishing the job and push you over the edge. Don't take it personally. It's what they're supposed to do. It's amazing how long determined parents can hang on to the end of their wits, when it's necessary.

Our daughter was fourteen or fifteen, strong-willed and a bit rebellious. Okay, she was a lot rebellious. She was a world-class door slammer. Our wedding anniversary had come and gone with no acknowledgment from her. If I remember correctly, she picked that day to cause more commotion than usual. I don't think she really forgot our celebration. She was simply too busy sorting out her own youthful trials and tribulations to remember. A week or so later, we found a handmade card, a big red heart on a piece of notebook paper. "Mom and Dad," it said, "Happy Belated Anniversary!"

> Roses are red
> Violets are blue
> No one can care as much
> As I do for you.
> Sorry (about everything), Amy

Her rough edges as a teenager, the difficult stage of development she endured, did indeed pass away. She is now the loving, gentle, patient parent of a beautiful baby daughter. We parents couldn't be prouder of her! She made it! And so did we! We'd do it again in a second, although we're thankful we probably won't ever have to. Raising teens is a job for younger, more energetic folk than for old grandparents like us.

2.
Growing Up Together

John the Baptist was a wise and courageous person. In order to allow Jesus' influence and ministry to grow, John graciously stepped aside. He publicly praised Jesus and identified him as Messiah, God's Anointed One. In the watershed third chapter of the Gospel of John, the Baptist says, "My joy has been fulfilled. He [Jesus] must increase, but I must decrease" (John 3:29c-30).

This could be a primary text for all parents of teens. As youth grow, parents must also grow. But there's a paradox here. The development of parents involves a decreasing role. I did not say a less important role, for parental involvement with teenagers is every bit as vital as it was for infants and children. It's just different. A gradual change occurs. As young persons acquire a greater sense of responsibility and develop a more mature capacity to make decisions, parents can and should back away. Don't go far. Stay close to offer support, to be a safety net in case of slips, to offer midcourse corrections when needed. But as the level of trust increases between parents and youth, the level of external control should decrease.

Knowing this truth and doing it are two quite different matters. It's not easy to watch your teen head toward what you know from experience to be certain failure. Yet those apron strings, which were long enough to go around your daughter or son in childhood, simply won't stretch far enough to encircle a teenager. If you try, be prepared for them to untie the knot as fast as you tie it. In a very real sense, the way for parents to hold on to youth is gradually to let go of them.

It's not always a comfortable position for parents. In those first twelve years of raising them, you had more direct control, or at least had that possibility. Then it began to change. They started pushing the limits. They wandered farther away from home for expanded periods of time. They asked for more room. "Give us space!" they demanded.

While we know intellectually that they need room for growth, it's still not an easy concept for our parental nature to accept. Though I'm not an ornithologist, I have an idea it's harder for adult birds to watch than for fledglings to teeter on the nest's edge. Youth, however, not only require bigger shoes and longer pant legs in order for their bodies to grow, they also need emotional space for their minds and spirits to expand.

One dominant characteristic of the teen years is growth. Rapid physical, psychological, and spiritual growth occurs, often at the same time. The process is both exciting and scary, quite impressive and very tiring for all parties involved. The same height that gives them a new perspective on life also causes them to trip over their own shoelaces. Awkwardness is an almost inevitable ingredient of the growth process. Don't expect everybody to look like a pink flamingo delicately perched on one graceful leg. A family with one or more teenagers is more likely to resemble the proverbial china shop with several bulls loose all at once.

Teens aren't the only awkward people in the family. Parents go through some major moments of disequilibrium, too, occasions of almost completely losing their balance. Perhaps they don't trip over shoelaces (folks of their generation were taught to tie them). They stumble instead over their tongues when inappropriate words tumble out of their mouths. They get tripped up from their inability to see the increasing maturity of their youth. Parents sometimes continue to view young adult off-spring as children. They speak to and discipline them accordingly. Family rules and expectations often don't grow along with the kids, at least not fast enough. What worked with a three- or six- or nine-year-old, will not be effective with most, if any, thirteen-year-olds.

Everybody's going to make mistakes along the way. There will be an impressive assortment of scrapes, lumps, and bumps. When one of our sons grew seven inches in something like eleven months, he kept running into our front porch light. He had the knots on his forehead to prove it. He kept forgetting how tall he'd suddenly become. It took awhile for his mental awareness to catch up to his newly acquired six feet, two inches of stature. So keep the bandages and ointments ready. Both of you will need them.

There will be scrapes and bruises of the soul as well. Be prepared for many energetic, animated, and occasionally heated discussions. Keep those lines of communication open and in good repair. Don't let anything clog them. Remove blockages immediately. Do not allow hurts and frustrations to hinder the exchange of ideas and experiences. Do not permit misunderstandings, disappointments, or suspicions to constrict the free flow of feelings.

Do you remember how Jesus began his youth? By gently, perhaps inadvertently rebelling, that's how. He stayed behind in Jerusalem to talk with the rabbis and leaders in the Temple. He wasn't deliberately disobeying Mary and Joseph. But he obviously hadn't informed them of his actions. They'd gone a day's journey before noticing his absence. That would be the equivalent in today's terms of traveling perhaps five hundred miles on the freeway. To their credit, his parents kept their composure even though it took three days to locate him. They were justifiably worried and did upbraid him for failing to ask their permission. But things were obviously different in first-century Palestine. We'd be frantic in these times, with good reason.

Jesus apparently didn't apologize, at least not in so many words. His reply was to ask two questions, "Why were you searching for me? Did you not know that I must be in my Father's house?" (Luke 2:49). Now how in the world would any parent in any historical period answer those questions? No wonder the scripture adds that Jesus' parents "did not understand what he said to them." Before we get too smug, let's admit we don't fully comprehend some of the responses of our youth today. But that's okay. We, like Mary and Joseph, can still be effective parents. We're told that "Jesus increased in wisdom and in years, and in divine and human favor" (Luke 2:52), not necessarily in that order. I figure two out of four would be an excellent average at any given time in a teenager's development. Over the span of seven years, parents will have ample opportunities to help their teenagers achieve all four.

Young people require room for exploration, for going on intellectual adventures and spiritual pilgrimages. They shouldn't have to demand it or constantly justify their need. Freedom ought to be granted to them in advance, well before they have to cause a commotion by pushing and shoving against boundaries that are too small. If you wish to guarantee that you will have rebellious youth, all you have to do is not grow with them. Just keep thinking of them as toddlers. Treat them like grade school children. You wouldn't dream of making them wear size five clothing. So provide them with adequate space for their inner growth.

I can't think of any living thing in the whole of creation that doesn't experience growing pains. Like a horse and carriage, like peanut butter and jelly, growth and pain go together. In fact, the more rapid the growth, the greater the travail is likely to be. In something as close and intimate as family life, the growing pains of one member are certain to become the pains of all members.

My suggestion is that parents seek to transfer those pains into "panes." It can be done. The awkwardness of teens has a humorous side to it. Laugh with them as often as possible. Use times of conflict as windows of clarification, to identify the sources of tension, to see more clearly the behavioral modifications everyone needs to make.

The teen years of one's children are perfect occasions for parents to produce the fruit of the Spirit. A bumper crop is quite possible. Why not aspire through those experiences to become a fully equipped spiritual person, having your tree of life loaded down with a harvest of "love, joy, peace, patience, kindness, generosity, faithfulness, gentleness, and self-control"? (Gal. 5:22). It can be a marvelous opportunity for the entire family to learn, grow, and become strong.

It helps to be gentle, kind, and compassionate when parents remember they are dealing with beings who are part child and part adult. Teens are perhaps direct descendants of those half-goat, half-human creatures in Greek mythology. You'll be a jump ahead if you expect them to act like they're twenty-five years old one day and two the next. Yes, it will keep you on your toes, which can become a rather tiring position unless you're a ballerina. But flexibility is not optional for parents of teens. As someone once said, "Blessed are the flexible, for they shall never be bent out of shape." Amen.

The pains become panes when parents are able to find new ways of experiencing fulfillment. Your joy in them was once the product of their pleasing you, of meeting your desires and expectations. You showed them the way and they followed. You offered advice and they accepted it. Now your joy as parents comes from new sources, from watching them find their own way, from encouraging them to make their own decisions. It may not be the direction you would have gone or the decision you would have made. But you learn to appreciate and honor their independence. You find satisfaction not in doing everything for them so much as in enabling them to do the things they're ready to do for themselves. Parents of teens will discover the joy of leading from the back of the pack. In some ways it's the satisfaction that comes from working yourselves out of a job. The ultimate goal of parenting is to relate to your children as one adult to other adults. Yes, you will always and forever be a parent. He or she will always and forever be your little baby. Yet because you have grown with them, you will come to see them as your equals, as your contemporaries.

The final, ultimate solution to this condition known as teenager is for them to mature, to grow into young adulthood. It doesn't necessarily happen by age twenty. It may occur earlier. Or it may take much longer. I've known people who were "thirty-teen" or "sixty-five-teen." The mere passage of time does not guarantee growth within. Maturation is much more than dropping the word *teen*. It involves incorporating a host of positive qualities.

It's important not to treat the teen years as nothing but turmoil, as a period of mostly negative attitudes and tremendous pressures. There will be tough times, a few struggles of the soul, and a number of conflicts. But teens possess strengths well worth preserving for the rest of their lives, qualities that would richly bless persons of all ages. I refer to the refreshing idealism of youth; to their ability to feel wonder and awe at life's mysteries; to their adaptability, their capacity to accept change as normal and healthy; to their talent for learning and assimilating new ideas; to their genius in sensing what is phony and unreal; to their aptitude for dreaming great dreams; to their amazing amounts of energy and enthusiasm.

Parents growing in skill and confidence while their teens grow in stature and maturity—it's not a new idea. But it's one that needs to be repeated in each succeeding generation. Accepting it requires a dose of parental humility, admitting that we don't have all the answers, acknowledging that there is always more to learn. If parents will listen, teenagers are willing and eager to remind them of this truth daily.

3.

Dealing with Real Fears Without Becoming Fearful People

*T*heir hearts are in the right place. They mean well. But I wish they'd stop saying it. I'm referring to folks whose children are no longer in the nest, who intend to be supportive and sympathetic. "Oh," they often say to those who are still actively parenting, "I'm so glad my kids are grown and gone. These are terrible times in which to raise a family. It was so much easier in my generation."

Perhaps in years gone by things were simpler. Pressures, complexities, and demands of family life have no doubt increased. Causes of genuine concern seem to be expanding rapidly. There are real fears, in far greater numbers today, which families must face and somehow survive. Parenting with confidence has never been readily achieved. But at this point in our history, the problems and anxieties are intense. Parents must safely guide young persons through such frightening realities as increasing drug experimentation and addiction, a constant stream of pornographic material, escalating crime, the lure of gangs, the haunting possibilities of cancer and AIDS, and an alarmingly high incidence of teenage suicide.

We are experiencing upheavals in our standards of sexual morality. Parents are not imagining when they tally the many sources of their worries: eating disorders, sexual activity at very youthful ages, teen pregnancies, alcohol abuse, peer pressure to cheat at school and to shoplift. The list of potential dangers is long. Because of extensive media coverage, including the visual impact of television, we are made instantly aware of national and global conditions as well. That's positive. We need to know. Yet it does add to the emotional burdens we carry in our hearts.

The major emphasis and sometimes excessive news coverage of terrible and tragic events is a very real source of fear. Daily we view graphic depictions of crime and violence. We read gruesome descriptions of our human capacity to hurt and destroy. It can create within us a constant uneasiness, an ever-present anxiety. We can come to the conclusion "it's a jungle out there," that the world is going to hell, that the safest thing may be to lock ourselves in our houses or apartments and never come out. Except even there we may not feel secure.

The question therefore is, "In a climate of fear, how do we raise confident, self-assured young people?" How can we inform them of all the perils and risks without turning them into anxious, fearful persons? It can be done. Parents can prepare their children by equipping them to see the world as it really is, a place of serious problems as well as marvelous possibilities; of ugliness as well as wondrous beauty; of disease, hunger, and poverty as well as health and abundance; of terror and tears as well as joy and laughter.

The key ingredient in showing them the way toward confident living is honesty. Parents must talk openly about their very real concerns and not hide their apprehensions. These should be shared not in an alarmist manner, not with the pulling of hair and gnashing of teeth but in a context of calmness and rationality. The primary source for young persons learning to be hopeful and productive is the way their parents and other role models live day by day. If adults adopt and follow a philosophy that life is basically, fundamentally good; that the positives far outweigh the negatives; that the future is bright with hope, their witness will be potent and contagious.

This is an age-old dilemma. Since the dawning of history, parents have had to equip their offspring with inner strength and confident attitudes in order for them to prosper in a world fraught with danger. The apostle Paul addressed the basic solution to this problem in his letter to the Philippian church. "Finally, beloved, whatever is true, whatever is honorable, whatever is just, whatever is pure, whatever is pleasing, whatever is commendable, if there is any excellence and if there is anything worthy of praise, think about these things" (Phil. 4:8).

Parents ought not minimize the possible problems, but they must also maximize the potential power. They should teach about the consequences of wrong choices, being careful never to motivate by fear. A solid and positive moral foundation must be established and faithfully maintained; namely that the universe is a friendly, fair, and good home in which to live and grow. Young persons need to be fully informed, always in the context of acceptance and love.

Jesus once said to a group of listeners, "You will know the truth, and the truth will make you free" (John 8:32). Education is the answer rather than isolation, proper preparation rather than panic. We're not talking about applying a sugar coating or wearing rose-colored glasses, just telling the truth—plain, simple, and unvarnished—and speaking it to them with respect in an atmosphere of trust. Ignorance is never bliss. Ask an ostrich which part of its anatomy is exposed and vulnerable to attack when its head is buried in the sand. In the field of mathematics, we're taught that any number times zero is always zero, no matter how big the original number. Living in fear does the same to our souls. It cancels out the positive experiences and negates the beauty and the joy.

There are varieties of ways to help teens achieve a balanced perspective on the problems and possibilities of life. One is to introduce the pitfalls to them in small doses. Be careful not to back up the dump truck and unload it all at once. It's easy for us, even for experienced, mature persons, to feel overwhelmed by the scope and sheer number of problems facing our world. I suggest letting youth deal with only a few problems at a time. If, in addition, they're facing personal or family difficulties, try to shield them a bit from community, national, and global troubles. Teens have their own unique worries, too, which may not seem earthshaking to adults. Nevertheless, they're very real to them. Respect them and try not to "pooh-pooh" their concerns. Be tender. You can be honest without being overly blunt. Let there be periods of rest and recreation, times of happiness between the tough experiences. Excessive worry in teenagers won't solve anything and likely will be detrimental to their physical and emotional health.

Assist them in biting off an amount they're able to chew and digest. It's analogous to the process when a teen gets his or her driver's license. As parents, we can offer greater freedom and responsibility as their experience and skill increase. After they pass their test, youth often want to take the car out for a spin, go over to a friend's and brag about how they aced the whole thing, how they weren't scared at all. That's fine. But parents have a perfect right, even a responsibility, to ask for an E.T.H.—expected time home; to set limits, such as no friends in the car at first, no out-of-town driving; and night driving only by permission. Youth may not accept it gracefully, although they'll eventually understand the rationale.

As their abilities improve and their confidence increases, parental trust in them will increase as well. They can be given more latitude, like taking buddies to a football game, making a short trip to a youth rally in a nearby city, going out in the evenings with a boyfriend or girlfriend. By the time they're ready to graduate from high school, they're capable of handling just about any situation on the highway, and parents can feel relatively secure in letting them go anywhere. Of course, you never completely stop worrying, even when they're grown and gone from home, married, or have their own business. Prayers seem to rise of their own accord from parents' souls when their children are traveling.

Parents can provide youth with a solid base from which to operate in the big world. When difficulties arise, when hurts happen, young people have a place of solace, a sanctuary where they can sort out their observations, talk through their feelings, and make sense of their confusion. Their coping mechanisms need time to develop along with their physical bodies, intellects, and spiritual lives.

To adequately equip young persons to deal with real fears, parents should employ all available resources. I remember as a youth how my father used trips in the car to share ideas, offer inspiration, and listen to my inner stirrings. When he had a particularly sensitive issue to discuss, he'd find an occasion when the two of us were alone in the car. It was there, for example, he introduced sex education to me and cautioned me about experimenting with alcohol and drugs.

It's important to take advantage of those serendipitous moments that happen in every family. When they first arrive home from school, talk about the stresses and disappointments they've experienced while the memories are still fresh. Nearly every day they see things that unsettle and upset them, just as you do. When they share those things, listen. Listen. Listen. Who cares if dinner is a half hour late? And maybe your colleagues could do without you for that evening meeting or for one night's play in the bowling league. There's never enough time in raising a family. So when those special, unscheduled opportunities pop up, grasp them. It may be at mealtime, in the middle of your favorite TV show, or just before they go to bed. Those occasions must be used at that very moment or perhaps be lost forever. Timing is critical. A few minutes later, your young person's feelings and needs may have changed dramatically. They may no longer be as eager to share what's in their hearts.

Pay attention to newspaper headlines and television news. They present events, sometimes admittedly with sensationalism, which are significant sources of our anxieties and fears. Discuss your own feelings as you read and watch. A sentence or two will often do. Long-winded sermons or lengthy lectures aren't needed. In fact, they're usually turnoffs, not only for youth but also for those of all ages. Keep moral pronouncements brief. The important thing is to get to the feeling level. Facts are facts are facts. Emotions are where our fears live, where the turmoil and insecurities build. And patient, interested, nonjudgmental listening is the best method I know for uncovering a young person's deepest feelings.

Planned discussions are also helpful, although they should be used sparingly and reserved for the biggest issues, those that should not be postponed. The benefit of scheduling appointments for family discussions are several. First, you aren't reacting to an immediate and pressing problem when emotions may be running high. It permits a reasonable, calm approach that produces more light and less heat. Second, it clearly communicates that you consider the particular issue to be important. You have set aside time to deal with it and made the effort to discuss it when family members can be present. With today's hectic family pace, that itself is a major accomplishment. Finally, you've called the meeting and are therefore looked to for guidance. It's your agenda. That doesn't mean you're the big boss and are free to dominate and dictate. Keep it a democratic gathering. It does, however, permit you to set the tone and offer helpful guidelines.

Along with talking about the fears, take action, do something together to make a positive difference in your neighborhood or community. It doesn't have to be on a grand scale. Mow an older person's lawn. Do what the family across the street from my eighty-year-old mother did. Their older daughter faithfully placed her garbage can at the curb every Monday evening, then put it back in the garage the next day as soon as school was over.

Her younger sister came for frequent visits, went walking with her, and brought in her mail. It was a mutually beneficial arrangement. They were being a wonderful help to a person in need. And she shared with them a lifetime of inner strength and courage.

One family may not be able to solve our society's entire crime problem, but they can make their own neighborhood a safer, friendlier place. Instead of simply bemoaning the world's sorry state of affairs, take action. It has an energizing effect. Yes, you should talk things through. Discuss all the issues in detail. Then as parents and youth, roll up your sleeves and get to work. Do something to restore creation's beauty, to help someone in need, to teach others the values you cherish.

Finally, take advantage of every available spiritual resource. Prayer should be a staple item in every parent's life. It doesn't have to be of the eloquent, formal variety. Parents of teens seldom have time or energy for such things, except when worshiping in church. One-liner prayers can be just as effective:

"Lord, help!"

"Oh God, I need an extra dose of patience and I need it now!"

"Dear Creator, give me a sign, even a small one, that 'This too shall pass.'"

Moments of quiet meditation are very helpful. Hum or whistle a favorite hymn. It has power to settle nerves and calm spirits. The scriptures are chock-full of words of courage and inspiration. My all-time, top-of-the-charts favorite is a message from the wise old Paul to a young Timothy. The biblical record doesn't indicate that Timothy was a parent, but I can't help wondering. "I want to remind you," advises the apostle, "to stir into flame the strength and boldness that is in you. . . . For the Holy Spirit, God's gift, does not want you to be afraid of people, but to be wise and strong, and to love them and enjoy being with them" (2 Tim. 1:6-7 TLB). If parents could lead young persons to live according to this text, what a precious gift it would be!

4.
Touchlove

T hankfully I have long since forgotten the cause of the argument. It may well have been an imagined slight. My anger, however, was real and in abundant supply. I'd had a conflict with a teenage son just before dinner. I sat in my chair at the head of the table, glowering. My appetite, which had been ravenous moments earlier, was totally gone. Fascinating how feelings of hostility seem to affect even one's taste buds.

He approached me from behind, but I knew it was him. I could tell from the sound of his steps. Had I been looking in his direction, I couldn't have seen much anyway through my beady, squinty eyes. Instead of brushing by me as he usually did on his way to his place, he paused, put his hands on my shoulders and began massaging. A football player and weight lifter, he had a strong grip. With each rubbing motion I could feel my anger dissipating. In spite of myself, I experienced compassion and forgiveness. His touch seemed to heal my annoyance and release the love in my heart. It set me free to reach toward my son and become an emotional and spiritual part of my family again.

That evening as we held hands and said grace together, it was for me more than a repetition of rote words. I meant it when we prayed, "God is great, God is good, let us thank him for our food." Quietly but with conviction, I added, "Let us thank God for touching and forgiveness and being family."

Touch at its best tries always to give itself with love. Love at its highest looks for a way of tenderly touching. It gives rise to a newly coined word in my vocabulary: *touchlove*. It requires changing only one letter, but it's a world apart in attitude and approach from toughlove, that well-known style of parenting. Yes, love is tough. Its power and strength, however, are not brittle and unbending.

Love is never mean or small or exclusive. It is always kind and expansive and inclusive. Love is toughest when it acknowledges its weakness, most powerful when it is vulnerable, truly potent when it yields its prerogatives. Love's forcefulness is demonstrated by gentleness, revealed in patience and persistence, offered in freedom. Love never ends. It simply will not go away, not in our loneliest hours, not when we're consumed by anger, not even in our deepest grief. Love abides. And touch is one of love's most important and wonderful vehicles of expression!

Touch is a way parents of teens can communicate their concern and love nonverbally. When word meanings change from one generation to the next, when emotions run strong and our thought processes fail, we need to use alternative forms of making contact with one another. Body posture, eye contact, tone and volume of voice are among the signals we send. We may offer gifts of flowers or candy, write letters, mail cards. But of all the methods of communicating without speech, I like touch best. It bridges the gap between language barriers. It reaches across differences in age, race, belief systems, political views, and denominational affiliation.

Touch is an absolutely necessary tool for parents, even from before birth when hands and ears are placed on the expectant mother's tummy. Touch helps us find our composure when we've lost it. We can count to ten through clenched teeth, go for long solitary walks, practice deep breathing exercises and sigh multiple times. We can and should pray for inner peace and outward calmness. I personally find digging in the garden or flower beds beneficial to my emotional health. But touching another human being is probably the ultimate way of healing and restoring a broken relationship.

I like being touched. It's not just gravy. It's the main course. Touch is not an extra added attraction but a necessity. I need hugs and handshakes, back rubs and squeezes. And I'm not ashamed to admit it. It's easier, I must admit, to touch pets, babies, and grandparents than most teenage family members. The latter may be awkward about it because they've grown so fast physically. They're no longer small children needing safety and protection.

Their striving for independence may cause parental touch to have a double message. On the one hand youth acknowledge their desire to feel loved and accepted. On the other hand they resist touch if it conveys even a hint that a parent still considers them children. Perhaps we might learn to touch young people in the same manner we do infants. Touching babies is a nonthreatening situation. There are no hidden agendas, no subtle lectures or moral messages. Holding a tiny one is basic stuff, touch that's pure and completely honest.

The Creator intends us to be touchers and "touchees." Why else were we given long arms with hands and fingers on the ends? They are handy for gathering and eating food, throwing baseballs, brushing teeth and combing hair, and for driving a car. But their most sublime purpose must be to touch people. When we were all part of a single lump of clay, mingled together in the dust of the earth, we were constantly in contact with every other potential life. Now as separate entities, as unique personalities, we must make an effort to touch others. We must take the risk of reaching toward them.

The problem for many teens is that they have ambivalent feelings about parental touch. They will no longer tolerate condescending pats on the head. When they want to hug you, they don't grab you around the knees or waist as they did in childhood. Youth are able to look you in the eyes and put their increasingly large hands on your shoulders. And some of them, the tall ones, look down on you and may have the urge to pat you on the top of your head. Parental touch must respect their newly found abilities, their increased need for privacy, and their growing sense of independence.

An appropriate way to touch a youngster may not be appropriate for a youth, unless they first invite you to do so. Tickling under the chin, for example, while making "gitchie-gitchie-goo" sounds is obviously out. So is pinching their cheeks. What was suitable for a two-year-old will probably not be so for a young person of fourteen. Some forms of touch depend on the individuals involved. There are teens who would die of embarrassment from holding hands with a parent in public. Other youth would consider it a normal and pleasant activity. Parents need to be constantly aware and sensitive to their teens' needs, which incidentally may radically change from moment to moment. Do not assume that your youth's willingness to be touched today will be the same tomorrow. Therefore, ask permission. It doesn't have to be a formal request. Learn how to read the signals. Know when and where certain types of touch are acceptable to the young people in your family.

When we are most unlovable is often when we most need to be touched. This is especially true with youth. Parents need to remember this and take the initiative. Reach out with kindness and compassion. You may be rebuffed. If so, bide your time. At least let them know you care. And don't take a teenager's initial resistance as a permanent, for-all-time-and-eternity refusal. An hour later, or a week later, or maybe not for a year, but down the road somewhere they'll want your touch. When that happens, don't be stubborn. Offer a hug and put your whole self into it.

Sometimes simply making the effort to touch is enough. When I have little fits of self-centeredness (and teens don't have a corner on this market), I display the sharp parts of my body. My elbows protrude more than is necessary. My chin juts out. I am not a very cuddly human being. Yet I need someone who loves me to find a way through my barriers and with a kind touch, reconnect me to my sisters and brothers on this planet. Teens require and deserve the same effort.

Since my own children are grown and gone, I can only say what I might do if I could parent again. If I could start over with child rearing, I would touch more, a great deal more. As much as humanly possible, I would touch always in positive and affirming ways. I would try never to withhold touch as a method of punishment. It is far too precious a gift to refrain from offering no matter how tense the circumstances or difficult the conflict.

The Creator constantly touches us through creation, through wind and rain and snow, with soil and water and plant life. It's an essential ingredient in our lives. Other of God's creatures understand this need. As I sat one warm spring day at our weather-beaten picnic table, trusted cat Henry rubbed against my leg, leaving a patch of fur on my pants. He is never reluctant about telling me of his need for touch. He's very direct about it. "Here's my body," he communicates, "pet me, scratch me behind my ears, listen to me purr."

What silly folks we humans are. We crave physical, emotional, and spiritual touch, but we act cool and distant. We don't just come out and honestly say, "I need to be touched." Perhaps it's why we flock to sporting events and concerts where throngs of people push and pull us. We're surrounded by touch and caught up in the noise and excitement of the event. We feel at one with others in the crowd. Maybe it's part of the reason youth like to listen to such loud music. It somehow touches them all the way down to their toes. Their entire bodies reverberate from the sound.

Touch is capable of being tough or tender, mean or kind, imprisoning or freeing. Be very aware that touch can be manipulative, controlling, and abusive. It can be wonderfully healing or terribly hurtful. It all depends on our motives. At its highest, it becomes touchlove in every relationship, including family life. Certain individuals and families are more comfortable with touch. It seems to come naturally for them. Yet among those who are more shy and hesitant, touch can still be sweet and lovely.

I yearn to give greater physical expression to my joys, my sorrows, and to the full range of my emotions in between. As I grow older and have less physical stamina, I become more aware of my dependence on others and of my finite nature. I need to touch and be touched. When someone tickles me, I forget my cares and woes and become childlike again, complete with wiggles and giggles. When I'm caressed, I can purr as loudly as any cat. When I'm held in a loving embrace, the whole universe seems secure.

Touch affirms us. It tells us we belong, we're secure, we're part of a loving community. If humanity were to lose the gift of touch, we might as well drift off alone on an Arctic ice floe. We're meant to live together in families, in towns and cities; to work together in jobs and professions; to join service clubs, school organizations, and churches. And in each and every one of them, to make contact with persons, to touch. Teens need touch! And so do their parents. One of the wonderful things I've noticed about touch is that when you give it, you can't help receiving it, too.

5.
Getting Upset for the Right Reasons

*P*arents of teens who try to do their best, who give themselves wholeheartedly to the task, who truly care about their offsprings' welfare, are going to get upset. It's not a matter of will they or won't they. The questions are rather When? How often? Over what issues? For how long? It really is all right to be bent out of shape sometimes, to have your nose out of joint or whatever phrase you choose to use.

It was permissible for the prophets of Old Testament times. People expected it of them. They regularly got upset about their nation's unfaithfulness to God. Their reasons for being perturbed were never trivial. The prophets always responded to just and righteous causes. Amos and Jeremiah, Isaiah and Jonah weren't simply blowing off steam. They weren't being cantankerous or acting from selfish motives. They addressed faults and failings of persons that, if left unchecked, would almost surely lead to the destruction of their society.

In like manner, when parents of adolescents get upset, it needs to be for the right reasons. Before listing those, however, let's discuss some of the wrong ones. Do not make a federal case out of their failure to hang up clothes or put them neatly in the dresser. Yes, it looks tidy when they do. Yes, not doing so might lead to additional lapses in neatness and orderliness. But contrary to popular opinion, cleanliness is not next to godliness. In fact, it has nothing whatsoever to do with it. I imagine that the first disciples were a ragtag bunch of individuals who didn't use deodorant, usually had dirty feet, and maybe had holes in the knees of their blue jeans or whatever it was they wore in the first century.

Cleanliness is a desirable trait, an admirable quality. It does make pleasant social contacts. But greasy hands, wax in the ears, fuzz in the tummy button, or dandruff on the scalp do not disqualify persons for admission into the kingdom of God. Perhaps we might not choose to sit next to them on the church pew, but spirituality is a condition of the soul, not of the flesh.

I feel very strongly that parents shouldn't blow a gasket over things such as a young man's leaving the toilet lid up, a teen's not putting the milk carton back in the refrigerator, or failing to turn the lights off, using all the hot water during a lengthy morning shower, or a multitude of other minor aggravations. If your teen is usually responsible, being fifteen minutes late for an agreed-upon return isn't grounds for a major confrontation. Mention the tardiness but don't belabor it. It's quite permissible to discuss these things in a reasonable and calm way. Disciplinary action isn't necessarily required. Of course, youth may consider being talked to by parents as a mild form of punishment in itself.

I confess as a parent I did not and still do not always practice what I preach, including this advice I'm presenting on these pages. Our six children would no doubt add an enthusiastic "Amen!" to that. I let the small stuff get to me more often than I care to remember. I forgot that warm, loving relationships are far more important than clean, tidy rooms; that clutter on their floors is much to be preferred to emotional messes with their parents or siblings.

Our motives for getting upset as parents are the key variables. Make certain the reasons are big ones, significant and worthwhile. Learn to look the other way when it's a trifling matter, when it's mere peanuts. The purpose of being agitated isn't to make a teenager feel badly. It must never be aimed at detracting from his or her self-esteem, and should not contain the tiniest hint of condemnation. Getting upset requires a serious expenditure of energy, so when it happens, make it count for something. A parent's intentions must be to offer correction, to keep a young person from harm, to teach, and to protect them from the hurtful forces in the larger world that might limit or even ruin their chances for a productive life. Try not to lose your credibility with teens by getting upset for minor, insignificant causes.

If God and the angels do give a final exam in the life beyond this life, I know for a certainty what will not be on it. We shall not be asked, "Did you make your bed every morning before breakfast? Did you eat all your peas and carrots before you had dessert? How often did you clean beneath the stove? Did you change your socks and underwear every day?" I'm convinced the questions will rather concern the quality of our relationships, our willingness to give and serve, the depth of our compassion, the joy and comfort we brought to others. We shall not be asked, "Did the color and pattern of your shirt always match that of your pants? Was your hairdo ever more than three years out of style?"

We may well be asked, "Were you honest and fair in your business dealings? Did you treat poor and rich people equally? Did you love others for who they were on the inside and not according to any external characteristics such as skin tone, language, manner of dress, money in the bank, or place of residence?" If there is a heavenly entrance exam, it will surely include, "Were you true to your own best self, and to the best of your ability did you follow the leading of God's Spirit?"

Being a parent does not mean ceasing to have strong feelings, or biting one's tongue and never expressing your joys and disappointments. You have a perfect right to reveal the hopes and fears that come with the territory of parenting. True, there's no justification for dumping negative emotions on anybody else, family or not. But there is every reason to share your feelings freely, honestly, and openly with those you love and trust, including all children and youth in your midst. When parents explain their deep-seated beliefs and commitments; express those things on which they base their commitments and decisions; and describe the factors that form the very foundation of their lives, teenagers will respect them, but don't expect them to clearly verbalize their admiration.

Do not anticipate passing on intact to your children the entire moral structure of your generation, any more than you will hand down your exact musical tastes, particular eating habits, or trendy clothing styles. It won't happen. Thank goodness for that! What a boring world this would soon become if nothing ever changed and we were a society of people who look, think, and act alike.

You should and can accomplish something far more significant with your children. You can model for them a way of life. You have the capacity to demonstrate the power of holding to strong views, the vitality that comes from believing in God's truth with "all your heart, and with all your soul, and with all your mind" (Matt. 22:37). Parents and teens share many common views. Their attitudes may be quite similar to yours. Their respective philosophy on life may be very compatible. But a word of caution: don't expect all goals, values, and hopes between you and your young person to be one and the same. You've grown up in different times. The events that shaped your life and theirs are unique to each of you.

Teens really do want parents to be true to their own convictions. They may act embarrassed when parents behave like old fuddy-duddies. I suspect that's how it's always been since the days of Adam, Eve, and their rowdy clan. And I hope that today's parents, even when they grow impatient and are ready to demand obedience, will yet permit young persons to be faithful to their deepest nature, will expect them to be true to their individuality, will encourage them to think their own special thoughts and feel their own emotions.

The trick is to know what issues are worth getting upset about; which ones deserve taking a stand and defending with all your parental energy. Then parents need a ton of wisdom in order to know how to use those moments positively. Referring to the ancient prophets again, they looked to God for guidance in such matters. They were truth tellers and not particularly concerned about whether their listeners agreed with everything they said. They proved to be very creative in the methods they employed. They waxed eloquent. Thousands of years later, their words are still potent and have a delightful poetic lilt. They wrapped their truths in vivid images and clever parables. They knew how to dramatize their message and thus get through their listeners' myriad defenses.

Parents of youth face the same problems. The objects of their wisdom come complete with built-in skepticism and resistance. Teens may immediately discount anything and everything Mom and Dad say. So the old folks have to be creative. Tell a story. Read poetry. Refer to a popular movie. Unfortunately, precisely when we most need a good command of language is when we're most likely to lose it; for example, when we're muddled and frustrated.

Getting perturbed, bothered, and bewildered happens to parents with children of any and all ages. It's normal. When those kids are teens, expect such feelings to visit on a regular basis. Figure on receiving the maximum daily dose of upsetting experiences. Therefore, take proper care of yourself as a parent. If you won't do it for yourself (be assured, you DO deserve it), then do it for their sakes. Eat well; get adequate exercise and rest; read and reflect; pray and worship. Practice on-the-job relaxation. If you aren't able to get away often, use those brief moments for yourself. Close your eyes and breathe deeply. Learn how to sigh well. Think pleasant and kindly thoughts. Remember your various family members by name in prayer.

When you're flustered and rattled, check to see if your ears remain open while your mouth is moving. It's possible to listen while you talk, including hearing the tonal qualities of your own voice. Be alert for the sounds of nagging, whining, and badgering. They're fairly obvious. When upset, strive for a vocal tone that's open and free, that has kindness woven through each and every phrase. Getting upset does not mean withdrawing from social interaction. Parents can be agitated as all get out and yet be compassionate, approachable, available, and loving.

Remember, human parents are going to get upset. So don't expend too much effort feeling guilty when you do. What truly matters is not so much how you feel as what you do with those feelings, the way you act on them. Take a page from those prophets of old and be creative, caring, and wise. Put your concern for the audience above your own needs. Make certain that when you're really bent out of shape it's over major issues and for the right reasons.

6.
From Night Lights to Porch Lights

We used to wear out night light bulbs on a regular basis. We had a minimum of one small light in each child's bedroom and one in each bathroom. They were on from shortly after dusk to well after dawn. I put in a large supply of those seven-watt bulbs. You never knew when a middle-of-the-night emergency might occur.

When our children became teenagers, night lights fell into disuse and gathered dust. Sixty-watt bulbs were what needed frequent replacement, many in the outside fixture by the front door. The porch light was on continuously from early evening until the wee hours of the morning to show the teen members of our family the way back, to provide them a welcome home.

Through the years Mom and I became almost as good at watching and waiting as that old light, except it never grew impatient and worried or said a reproachful word. It faithfully kept a silent vigil, cheerfully greeting but never scolding no matter what the hour. I'm sorry to confess that we weren't always so gracious.

Waiting, of course, is part of life. No one is immune from having to stand in lines at grocery stores, banks, movie theaters, and busy fast-food restaurants. Cooling one's heels is a legendary pastime while sitting in doctors' offices. All these pale by comparison to what parents of teens must endure. Of course parents want their young people to be active and involved. But when that happens, waiting becomes an inescapable part of the deal. In raising teens, you don't simply add to your waiting. You better get out that trusty calculator and start multiplying.

Jeremiah tells us in the Scriptures, "It is good that one should wait quietly for the salvation of the LORD" (Lam. 3:26). The prophet's advice indicates that it's difficult for folks like us to wait for God to act. How much more difficult it is for us to wait upon mere people; people who get tired, make mistakes, and procrastinate. Hardest of all, perhaps, is waiting for teens. They make parents wait in wind and rain and sleet and snow, with dinner getting cold on the table, with the car idling at the curb and the gas gauge on empty, when you're already late for a meeting and you're both the chairperson and the program.

Not only that, teens aren't likely to reciprocate when it comes to waiting. They expect you to wait patiently for them with no complaints. It's okay for Mom to sit fifty minutes double-parked at the movies while they play video games in the lobby, visit with their buddies, and munch on popcorn. But woe to Mom if she's two minutes late, even if the reason for her tardiness is that she got caught in a massive traffic jam, had two flat tires, and drove through an earthquake of 7.5 on the Richter scale.

I suppose this waiting for offspring starts at the very beginning. Babies decide on their own when to make an appearance in this world, often at the most inconvenient of times, like 3:00 A.M. when normal people, including the obstetrician, are sound asleep. One tiny little life manages to wear out, in addition to its mother, a father, several doctors, nurses, and grandparents, and a host of friends. Why should we expect things to improve when that baby grows up and becomes an adolescent?

There are a variety of styles of waiting. During the teen years of our six children, at one time or another I've tried them all. See how many you recognize and check those that apply.

Style No. 1: The famous SPLEEN VENT. The conversation between parent and teen is basically a monologue. The parent's mouth goes nonstop while the teen nods in mock agreement, looks totally bored, or mumbles things like, "Yeah," "Uh-huh," "Oh-h-h," and "Is that right?"

"Where have you been?" the parent says abruptly. "I've been waiting for hours! Do you think you're the only busy person in this family? Are you listening to me? I've got a million things yet to do today. Don't you ever think about anybody but yourself? Next time, young man [or woman], you can find your own way home." This goes on until the car pulls into the family driveway. Mercifully, it usually ceases when the car is in the garage and the engine is turned off. It solves nothing and serves only to make both persons feel guilty. The Spleen Vent is not approved by the American Council of Parents Who Wait for Teens.

Style No. 2: The TIGHT LIP approach. This involves several icy parental stares at the youthful offender, followed by an absolutely unintelligible conversation, including the worn-out phrase, "If I've told you once, I've told you a thousand times."

The other morning when I was rather cranky from having to wait, I turned to our youngest son and those words just tumbled out of my mouth by themselves. I was powerless to stop them. "If I've told you once, I've told you a thousand times. Don't keep me waiting. Punctuality, you know, is a virtue!"

"I know, Pop," our youngest child once replied, "but you're wrong about one thing. According to my calculations, you're now up to 1,377 times on that particular meaningless statement." I remember employing the Tight Lip method when our then fourteen-year-old son wanted a ride to the Training Station, a local fitness center. "It's a beautiful day, young man. Why don't you walk or ride your bike?" It seemed a perfectly logical choice to me.

"Oh Dad, you just don't get it, do you? This is Tuesday and it's not my day to work on legs. That's Wednesday. This is when I build my upper body; you know, my arms and chest." He showed me a bulging biceps to prove his point. Silly me. How could I have been so dumb? I gave him a ride but my lips were blue from lack of circulation by the time we got there.

Style No. 3: The REVERSE PSYCHOLOGICAL PLOY. I don't recommend this method unless you're an accomplished actor or actress. A certain amount of dramatic flair is required to pull it off. You've waited in the car for hours. It's below zero weather. Your hands are frozen solid to the steering wheel and your breath has formed icicles on the rearview mirror. Your son or daughter finally returns. The first words out of your teen's mouth aren't "Hi Mom, thanks for being so patient!" Not even close. It's more like, "Hurry up, Mom, I've got to get home in time to watch *Leave It to Beaver* reruns. And I'm starved. What's for dinner?"

Nevertheless, you smile and say, "Thank you for making me wait here outside. I really enjoyed being turned into a 130-pound block of ice. Isn't that blizzard out there the most beautiful thing you've ever seen?" The Reverse Psychological Ploy cannot be used too often without seriously diminishing its results and your parental credibility. Teens quickly see through even Oscar-winning performances.

Style No. 4: The LAUGH AND THE WORLD LAUGHS WITH YOU method. Humor can defuse potential conflict, even an explosive situation, although it must be genuine and truly funny. Biting sarcasm is out. The best humor is woven into a parent's personality. It's sort of like laughter leaven, which lightens the entire loaf of family life. Subtle humor is often the most effective. Your teen has kept you waiting interminably. When he eventually decides to grace you with his gangly presence, you exchange a few pleasantries. Partway home you turn toward him and say, "Have you read any of Washington Irving's works lately? I have in mind a story called *Rip Van Winkle*. I believe Mr. Irving used me for his inspiration, since at latest count I've lost over twenty years of my life waiting for you."

"How can that be, Dad? I'm only thirteen." Don't let him fool you with his skill in new math. Or how about a reply like this?

"I'm thinking of contacting the folks who publish the Guinness books to see if they have a category of waiting for teenage daughters. If so, I'm a cinch for the world record."

Whatever styles a parent uses, it's good to anticipate the waiting. Offer them pleasant and creative lessons in punctuality. Impress upon teens the importance of being on time. Remind them that there are occasions, for example, when someone is in trouble or hurt, that a few minutes can make a big difference. Do not naïvely assume that your young person will be an exception to the rule and will always be on time. You'll simply set yourself up for frustration and trouble when he or she is not. Decide in advance how you're going to handle the waiting. You may react in a very different manner than what you planned. At least you will have made the effort, and next time you might actually pull it off.

Waiting is hard work. Harder than splitting a cord of seasoned oak. Harder than scrubbing the bathroom fixtures before company comes. So don't be fooled. But waiting need not be wasted time. It can be redeemed in hundreds of positive and creative ways. No matter how anxious or upset you get, it will not hasten a teen's return by even the tiniest of a microsecond. If you're like most parents, you're probably a long way behind on sleep. Try resting. Practice your deep breathing, preferably with your eyes closed. Relax. Take a nap. Give your body a break. Snore if you wish. If you're sitting in the car, roll up the windows and no one will hear.

Work on a task you've been unable to accomplish during the hustle-bustle of the day. Balance your checkbook. File your nails. Read a trashy novel or peruse the newspaper. Plan a week's menus. This last one pleases teens because they're always concerned about where their next meal is coming from and if it will be something they like. I often make entries in a journal, which I keep handy for such situations, although half the time I can never find a pencil or pen. Write cards and letters to friends and family members. Waiting goes faster if you don't feel that the time is lost and gone forever. Strive for a sense of accomplishment. Do something positive. Anything. You're serving as a chauffeur so behave like one. Get out there and polish the hood, wash the windows, check the oil, kick the tires. Above all else, keep busy.

I'll wager you're also behind on saying your prayers. Parents get precious little meditation time. Don't allow feelings of impatience to rob you of this peace and quietness. Close your eyes and if you don't immediately nod off, pray. Remember things you may have done wrong and ask for forgiveness. Offer prayers of thanksgiving that you have such a busy, active young person. Meditate on the joys of being a family, on the energy that comes from being part of a community, and on the beauty and glory of nature. Be grateful. Offer intercessions for people in this world who have waited far longer than you ever will just for scraps of food to feed their families. Do not, repeat, do not ever interrupt your silent prayers to look at your watch. If your car has a clock, I suggest covering it with masking tape until after your son or daughter has that twentieth birthday.

Other helpful spiritual and religious activities can be followed, such as humming or whistling old hymn tunes, although you should have a strong self-image because people may raise their eyebrows. "Oh, look at that poor woman. She's the parent of a teenager, you know. Pity what's happened to her."

When all else fails, philosophize while you wait. This is drastic action and is to be used only in dire circumstances. Reflect on how waiting is good for the soul, how suffering is an essential part of one's faith and helps us appreciate the desired result when it finally occurs. Waiting may be a reminder that we humans aren't so all-fired powerful, a lesson that there are some things we can never change. Our parental role may be simply to accept what happens and make the necessary adjustments. Or consider the possibility that waiting might actually be a blessing in disguise. It will likely have such a great disguise, however, it will take you awhile to notice.

I sometimes muse about how unfair it is for me to have to wait. I probably sound like Job of Old Testament fame, muttering to myself, "Why is this happening to me? What did I do to deserve such a fate? Woe is me." The answer comes quickly. I deserve every moment of waiting I'm required to do, and more besides. After all, my parents waited for me, Lord knows how long. They were so good at it I never even knew what they had to endure. I suppose it's a form of penance—the Almighty's way of balancing the generational scales of justice.

We might transform lives, make the world a happier place, and solve the major social problems of our age if we learned to see waiting as a gift to be opened rather than a burden to be borne. Well, maybe those claims are a bit ambitious. At the very minimum, it may calm our nerves and make us a pinch easier to live with. That's an excellent start.

Next time you're waiting for somebody, especially a somebody with that four-letter "T" word at the end of their age, memorize this text and repeat it as often as necessary: "Wait for the LORD; be strong, and let your heart take courage; wait for the LORD!" (Ps. 27:14). Good things do indeed come to those who wait and serve!

7.
Three Other
Important R's

*T*he traditional curricula of education, those famous Three R's: reading, 'riting, and 'rithmetic, are important. They're skills every young person must master in order to succeed in today's demanding times. Schools rightfully place emphasis on these intellectual disciplines. However, since they're learned skills and retained by the mind, they do not address issues of the heart. They cannot and are not intended to provide moral and spiritual guidance. Moral content is vital, perhaps even more so than these familiar Three R's, and must be regularly and faithfully taught to our children and youth. Without clearly defined values, all the technical abilities in the world become nothing more than interesting abstractions. Inner satisfaction, personal fulfillment, rich relationships, and a high quality of life absolutely depend on our intimate acquaintance with three other important R's: responsibility, respect, and reverence.

These are hard concepts to define and difficult to teach because they have no tidy handles. Older generations cannot neatly package their values and simply hand them to younger generations. Instead, mature persons must act as role models, set positive examples, live well, and behave justly. Measuring the results of teaching spiritual and moral values is impossible, at least with any precision. The seeds that are planted may not take root, grow, or bear fruit for years, even for decades. Yet we must keep witnessing to our values and continue honoring our moral commitments. We dare not waver. We may think they're not watching, that young persons don't even notice how we live and whether our actions match our publicly proclaimed values. But they do!

We need to instill a sense of *responsibility* in those who follow in our footsteps, and the primary place in which to accomplish this is the family unit. A responsible person is reliable, trustworthy, accountable, faithful, dependable. They carry through on projects and finish what they start. Responsibility includes being competent and capable, having a willingness to perform consistently at the highest possible level. It implies a caring for others and the desire to make a difference in people's lives.

Youth need to learn that responsibility isn't done only when they feel like it. It's a quality that will permeate their entire personality. Whether the task is great or small, they'll complete it with thoroughness and with attention to detail. It will be successfully done whether or not anyone is observing. Constant supervision isn't necessary for responsible persons. A genuine sense of responsibility comes from within a person, arising from motives of compassion and concern.

I remember well one of our family members, who as a teen simply could not or would not care for his room. His personal living space was the pits and had an odor to match. We as parents weren't terribly strict about how our children kept their rooms. We did, though, have certain minimum standards that we asked them to uphold. He never came close. Sweaty gym socks gathered mold on his floor. Dirty clothes covered every square inch of the place. Who knows what creatures lurked beneath those piles. He kept his door shut but we knew what it was like in there. The fumes seeping out gave him away. Perhaps we could have accepted his slovenly ways had he not blamed us when he couldn't find anything clean to wear. It was doubly hard to take given the fact that his room was right next to the laundry area.

All he needed to do was kick his dirty clothes out the door. We'd have gladly done the rest.

We expected better from him and continually asked him to act more responsibly. I'm sure he interpreted it as nagging, as "getting on his case." We saw it as asking him to practice the principles of basic hygiene. I won't lie and tell you he changed overnight. Some miracles unfold slowly. In fact, I think it took several months, if not years, but we were eventually victorious. It's usually preferable not to engage in matters that have a "somebody wins–somebody loses" mentality. But sometimes in parenting that's the way it has to be. He finally saw the wisdom of our ways, although I wonder if it had more to do with impressing girls than in pleasing his parents. What's the difference? The bottom line was he kept his room fairly clean. And now, ten years later, as a husband and father, he does his share of the housework, gladly takes responsibility for helping raise their three-year-old son, and even does some of the washing and ironing. It warms our hearts to see how far he's come. I'm certain we made our share of mistakes as parents, but occasionally we must have done something right.

Trickery and bribery are not effective methods of producing responsible behavior. Parental teaching techniques must be in character and consistent with the desired end results. The goals for teens are to become self-motivated persons, disciplined from within. I do not think it wise to pay children or youth for doing chores around the house or for getting good grades in school. If allowances are given, they should not be considered payment for tasks that ought to be freely done as a contribution to the family. Youth, like all of us, need to learn to work for the satisfaction of contributing to the whole.

They should read, study, do their homework, and strive for the highest attainable marks simply for the pure joy of learning. This may seem unrealistic given the pressures these days to succeed. But it is attainable. The purpose here is not just to achieve short-term results such as getting the dishes washed or earning an A in world history. Our aim as parents is to offer teenagers a lifetime blessing of becoming responsible, reliable people. It requires a greater expenditure of patience and energy to attain long-range goals. But it's well worth the effort! We want to believe that we're in this parenting business for the long haul.

Respect may soon be included on the endangered species list. It seems to be in increasingly short supply in modern society. The honor given to public servants and other authority figures has been seriously eroded. We don't have to agree with every decision made by teachers, school administrators, law enforcement personnel, or religious and political leaders. Nevertheless we can respect their position and pay tribute to their willingness to serve.

This loss of respect negatively impacts the role of parents. Children and youth no longer accept parents' opinions and directions because they're told to do so. Overall, that's a healthy direction. Parents and other authority figures must earn that respect. It keeps persons on their toes and makes them accountable for their actions. It can also motivate youth to grow and mature as they learn to think for themselves. It means more work for parents, having to explain their actions and requests. It marks the end of the authoritarian phrase, "Because I said so, that's why!"

Respect starts with the individual. If I do not believe in myself and properly care for my own body, if I fail to honor my own needs and follow my own dreams, I will find it difficult to love and respect others. Being respectful requires a strong self-image and no small amount of courage. If parents expect young persons to be respectful, they must in turn treat them with respect and take seriously their ideas, feelings, and wishes.

Developing an attitude of healthy respect among youth is crucial to the future of this planet. We must all learn to value the earth and its precious resources. A host of environmental problems exists that should raise our awareness, conditions such as littering and pollution, excessive consumption, the possible extinction of entire species, the very real threat of destroying rain forests for economic development, and the thousands of other ways we harm the delicate ecological balance of creation.

The critical concern seems to be with our level of caring. We have a problem of motivating people to take action. We know about the need to conserve and recycle. It's a matter of doing it. Along with learning the facts, we must come to respect this earth and to walk gently upon it. I know of no better method for passing on this attitude to young people than by practicing it ourselves. Lecture teens until your jaws are weary and you've run out of words. It won't matter. How you live is your best, most effective way of teaching. They'll see your respect for creation and for all life, or your lack thereof, and it will communicate more eloquently than tons of sermonettes.

I'm convinced that adolescent persons who respect them-selves, their own bodies, minds, and souls, are equipped to respect others. A teen who believes that his or her body is indeed a "temple of God" will be much more likely to take proper care of it. The greatest deterrent to drug and alcohol abuse is for youth to place a high value on their bodies and inner selves. The motivation for getting proper nutrition, adequate exercise, and all the requirements of a healthy body must come from within. Parents may and should suggest, teach, inform, sometimes even nag, and repeat the message of self-respect over and over again. But at some point, the importance of respecting their physical, mental, and spiritual selves becomes their responsibility. As in a relay race, parents and youth need to work on perfecting a smooth exchange of this value.

Children and youth can be taught to respect other persons' property, rights, and beliefs. They can learn to accept and honor persons from widely different cultures and ethnic backgrounds. We don't have to throw up our hands in despair. When we model this loving attitude for them, they will follow our example, especially when it's deeply felt and an integral part of our own lives. Our profound hope as parents is that respect for self, for others, and for the earth will become written on their hearts and become as natural and comfortable for them as breathing and eating, as sleeping and waking.

A sense of responsibility, an attitude of respect, and the final R, a feeling of *reverence,* are three wonderful gifts to offer young persons. Reverence is getting goose bumps from hearing great music or seeing the majesty of nature, from gazing at the stars all ablaze in the night sky or smelling a rose, from experiencing the mystery of birth. I was a fourteen-year-old lad when I first heard a symphony orchestra. My experience had been limited to small, rural towns in the northwestern United States. I had only listened on the radio or heard records of classical music. Nothing had prepared me for the sound of the Boston Pops in concert. Music filled every nook and cranny of that cozy high school auditorium. The acoustics were probably terrible but I never noticed. My teenage soul soared with every note of the violin section, thrilled to the brass, vibrated with the percussion and bass instruments. I was overwhelmed with joy. I can still hear it forty years later, can still remember how it felt to have my ears and toes and fingertips tingle.

It was a moment of reverence for me, of awe and wonder and delight. It was a sacred time in my life. Moses experienced this and much more when he encountered the burning bush at Horeb, the mountain of God. As Moses approached, God spoke. "Come no closer! Remove the sandals from your feet, for the place on which you are standing is holy ground" (Exod. 3:5). Mountain-top experiences may not occur often, but when they do they have the power and spiritual energy to change lives, even to alter the course of historical events. Youth are quite capable of having such experiences. Parents can't really plan or program them. These special events are gifts from the Creator. But parents can and should prepare their children and youth for receiving the blessings of God that await them.

Worship is a key ingredient. Formal worship may sometimes be boring for youth, yet even then it has spiritual value. When the Word of God goes forth, whether spoken or sung, it accomplishes its purposes. "So shall my word be that goes out from my mouth; it shall not return to me empty, but it shall accomplish that which I purpose, and succeed in the thing for which I sent it" (Isa. 55:11). Being together with others on the same journey of faith has a very positive influence. Encourage teens to regularly spend moments of quietness, to read and study the Bible, to find times for listening and wondering. In their usually noisy and sometimes tumultuous lives, teens may actually welcome opportunities for silence. This means, obviously, that you as parents cannot be constantly talking to them, either. Let there be spaces between your words, places for youth to rest and reflect.

Encourage youth to share their mountaintop experiences with you. Show interest when they tell their joys. And give them your blessing when they say their ears and toes and fingertips tingled. You'll know they've felt the touch of God's Spirit. Simply add an "Amen." While you're at it, you might want to take off your shoes, for this is holy ground upon which you walk.

8.
Blest Be the Binds That Tie

*W*hen they saw all those clothes hanging outside, our kids thought we were having a yard sale. "Not so," Mom and I explained, trying not to chuckle too loudly. "The dryer is broken so we're using our old clothesline."

"You mean you can actually dry clothes like that?" they asked.

"Of course you can. And everything smells so good from being in the fresh air." They went to the backyard for an inspection and were amazed by those little spring-loaded wooden devices that held the clothes on the line.

"What do you call them?" they inquired.

"Clothespins," we answered.

"Are they a new invention?"

"Heavens, no. They've been around for as long as we can remember."

"Oh, so they're really, really old, huh?"

"Very funny. By the way, if any of you have any more dirty clothes stashed away, you better take them to the laundry room right away." Half a ton of clothing suddenly, mysteriously appeared in a heap by the washing machine. When the next load was finished, I piled it in a plastic basket and headed toward the clothesline. Dave, our youngest, who was thirteen, followed along.

"Need any help, Pop?"

"Sure, Dave. Here's a bag of clothespins."

We worked silently together for a few moments; then he suddenly stopped, held up a pair of his underwear, and said with conviction, "I'm not hanging these on the line!"

"Why not?" I asked.

"Because all my friends in the neighborhood will see them, that's why. It would be embarrassing."

"But, Dave," I protested, "everybody wears such things. Nobody will even notice; and if they do, they won't care."

"I will," he said. We compromised and hid his unmentionables between the sheets and bath towels. That evening when I went out to bring the dry clothes inside, Dave's undergarments were nowhere to be found. It seems he removed them as soon as my back was turned. He dried them on the shower curtain bar in the downstairs bathroom.

It took several weeks and a number of trips to the hardware store to get the part and fix the dryer. Not only that, but the weather turned wet. Eight people and no quick way to dry clothes proved to be quite an inconvenience, especially for our teenagers, who must have a fresh towel every time they shower. And they have to shower at least twice a day.

We made it, and in the process discovered an interesting truth. We had fun, not just a little but a bundle of it. Sure, it was a challenge but we enjoyed it. We encountered a problem and together we discovered a solution. It was like taking the beloved gospel hymn, "Blest Be the Tie That Binds," and twisting the words around so they read, "Blest Be the Binds That Tie."

With determination and God's help, we can turn our troubles into triumphs, the binds we experience into blessings, our griefs into glories. And this is not simply wishful thinking. The apostle Paul shared this fact with the church in Rome. "Suffering produces endurance, and endurance produces character, and character produces hope, and hope does not disappoint us" (Rom. 5:3-5). In other words, family life problems can be used to our advantage. Working with one another can bring the various family members together in a combined effort to find answers. Getting out of binds provides strength and patience. Strength and patience give us character, making us individuals with humor and humility. And that means we ultimately become positive, pleasant, productive people.

Rather than avoiding conflicts and crises, it's better to take them head on. They can serve as important opportunities for learning and growth. We need to contend with the binds of modern family life until we've wrestled a blessing from them. Often when we look backward, the most difficult times, those tightest binds we were in, prove to have been among the best moments of our lives.

For example, when my wife, Ellen, and I were first married, things were tough. We were both students at Boston University, three thousand miles away from home, and poor as church mice. I remember hunting for coins in the creases of an old overstuffed chair when we wanted to buy ice-cream cones. The chair was particularly effective at parting people from their pocket change because its broken springs made the occupant sink down deep.

It wasn't easy, yet we had a ball! We enjoyed free concerts, long walks along the Charles River, autumn in New England, riding the subway, and soaking up the atmosphere in ancient church buildings and massive libraries. Being poor was actually a boon to our relationship. Others may have thought we were deprived. We never knew. We were too busy caring for each other and enjoying life to realize it. These were among the most romantic times we've ever had.

You and I don't have to be rich and famous, wonderfully accomplished or perfect to be good parents. In fact, striving for outward perfection can be quite a burden for us to bear. Expecting perfection from family members, especially teens, will produce all kinds of undesirable attitudes such as guilt, anxiety, and frustration. What matters in parenting is the honesty of our inner motives, the purity of our love, and the integrity of our personal values. When I reflect about the friends I've had over the years, the ones I feel closest to, those with whom I have had the sweetest ties aren't those who acted as though they were perfect. It's the ones who shared both their joys and their sorrows, their strengths and weaknesses. When persons allow others free access to their whole lives and don't pretend to be something they aren't, intimacy with them is possible.

Give assurances to the young people in your family that they can be fully human, can make mistakes and get into major binds, and it won't diminish your love for them. Demonstrate concretely that you're willing to "hang in there" with them. "Blest be the binds that tie" can be more than so many words, more than a clever but empty phrase. It can become a reality in families, churches, and communities. True, as children grow older, the binds they get into grow bigger, more complicated, and more expensive. When they're teens, solutions are more difficult to find but not impossible. In some aspects, the greater the effort required to solve problems, the greater the blessings to parents and youth. The apostle Paul expressed this truth when he wrote, "We know that all things work together for good for those who love God" (Rom. 8:28). He didn't claim that everything would automatically fall into place. He knew, as we do, too, that it requires work and prayer, as much perspiration as inspiration.

Agricultural experts tell us that apple trees do better when they have to work hard. When they have things relatively easy, when the weather is always mild and moisture is plentiful, trees spend too much time producing foliage. That is, they primp and preen and concentrate on their outward appearance. Considerable amounts of their energy go into looking good. But when trees face challenges, when winters are cold and spring is unsettled, their attention is focused on producing fruit. The apple crop is then of a higher quality. The fruit is tasty, crisp, and able to be stored for long periods of time. "Blest be the binds that tie" is apparently as true in the realm of nature as it is in our human relationships.

The Theory of Chaos is a current and exciting concept in the fields of mathematics and physics. In the last few decades of scientific thought, scholars have attempted to explain variations in the universe, random behavior in creation, and continuous turbulence in the cosmos. They have tentatively concluded that the outward order is not what it seems at first glance. There is structure and order but it is far more complex and involved than we ever imagined.

Chaos Theory may also hold true in our family connections, and extremely so when teenagers are present. Trying to establish order can be quite a challenge. Family members' hectic schedules may be nearly impossible to coordinate. To outsiders, it may seem to be total anarchy, complete confusion. But in today's active, busy society, that's rather normal. Family values are certainly under attack. There are pressures not experienced by families of only a decade ago. Yet deep inside the turmoil of family life is a mysterious order, felt by loving parents and experienced by their children.

Make no mistake about it, these are not easy days for families. We need, therefore, to see that the chaos has creative possibilities. The old patterns are rapidly changing. God is doing a new thing in our midst. And the basic building block of humanity, the family, is square in the middle of it. We need to help one another through these troubled times, seeking to discover the inherent patterns and power in them.

Don't give up on the family. Keep believing in young people. The future with all its predicaments, problems, fears, and dilemmas is bright with promise. "Blest be the binds that tie!"

9.
A Tender Topic: Discussing Their Sexuality

*F*or the rest of my days I will remember how his office looked that Saturday afternoon. I'd just turned sixteen and had been out on a date the night before in our family car. I'd returned rather late. Actually, it was rather early, as in the hours of early morning. My father requested an appointment with me soon after I straggled out of bed for lunch. I immediately knew something was up, something big. We discussed the usual problems while he sat on the edge of my bed, or at the kitchen table over a cup of hot chocolate. This must be really important.

With a certain amount of fear and trepidation, I trudged to his office. It was an impressive place with dark wood paneling and a massive old desk. Three walls were covered with bookcases, each crammed with thick and scholarly volumes. He indicated for me to sit. I sank into the chair with the leather seat cover that squeaked every time I squirmed. What did he want? If I was clever enough, could I talk my way out of whatever the problem was?

"Son," he spoke in somber tones, "you know something about bulldozers, don't you?"

"Yeah, I suppose so," I replied, wondering what in the world he was talking about.

"Well, a D-8 Caterpillar tractor is a pretty powerful machine. When you turn on the engine and get that piece of equipment cranked up, it's almost impossible to stop its progress, if you get my meaning." I didn't have a clue. I figured I must have missed a page in his fatherly playbook. Why would he call me to his office to discuss bulldozers? Maybe he was older than I thought. "So, young man," he continued, "it's better not to turn on that engine until you're capable of controlling it."

"Excuse me, Pop," I interrupted. "What's the point of this?"

"The blanket I found in the trunk of the car this morning, that's the point!"

"Oh, now I get it." What followed was a frank discussion of sexuality as it pertained to a teenage boy growing up in the late 1950s. My father went on to emphasize the joys and delights of human sexuality, but strongly suggested that I was not yet mature enough for the most intimate of male-female relationships. Ever since that afternoon I've gotten many a good laugh from recalling my father's famous "bulldozer lecture." It may have been a bit corny but it was effective. I heard the message and have never forgotten it.

Sexual suggestions and stimulation are everywhere around us these days, present for teens as well as adults. And it probably won't be going away anytime soon. In fact, it may well get worse before it gets better. We therefore need to educate, inform, and equip young persons as completely as possible in order for them to deal with their emerging sexuality. Not to do so leaves them at the mercy of both inward and outward forces that are exceedingly strong. They simply don't make a rug big enough on this planet to sweep teenage sexuality under its corner.

Sex is admittedly a tender topic for discussion but one we must discuss openly and frankly with teens. I'd far rather write about sexuality than talk about it face to face with someone, especially when that someone is in my own family. Even with all its media exposure, the raft of explicit public reports, and its constant use in advertising, sexuality is still a private matter for most of us. I always get a little flustered when the subject arises. I give myself a fairly good grade on my knowledge of sex, say a B-plus. But on my skill at talking to each of our children about it, I probably deserve a D-minus, if not a downright flunk.

However, there's really no avoiding it. As the old saying goes, "You can pay me now or you can pay me later." And payment later is always more costly. So parents need to talk with their teens about these matters. Go ahead, get embarrassed. Stammer if you must. Feel the redness move up your neck and watch your palms become sweaty. That's life. But talk with them about their sexuality. The flush in your face will soon drain away. Those stomach knots will eventually untie themselves. The introduction of the subject, that beginning sentence is always the most difficult. Once you get those first words out, the rest will flow more easily. I'm convinced teens want parents to share their knowledge and wisdom about sexuality. They don't want a lecture so much as to have a give-and-take discussion, perhaps including a bit of debate.

When talking about sexuality, speak the truth as you understand it and always with an attitude of compassion. Be sensitive to their needs. Don't volunteer more material than they're ready to hear and absorb. Listen carefully to their questions. Be kind but be honest. Parents should never lie to their children about sexuality, no matter what age the children are. Use correct anatomical terms. Tell the facts clearly. It's far better to be aboveboard with them about sex than to force them "undercover" in their search for knowledge. They're going to encounter all kinds of information in the big world out there, unfortunately much of it inaccurate and some of it completely false. Parents really don't want their family members learning about sexuality from dirty jokes in locker rooms, from reading so-called sophisticated magazines, from movie love scenes, or from the partial truths and shared ignorance of their peers.

And parents today don't want their youth repeating the kind of sex education I had. My father and his bulldozer analogy gave it a try. I give him credit for that. We had a number of helpful and informative visits on the subject. In the fifth or sixth grade at school, all we got was a dated filmstrip with a few boring diagrams, some basic biological facts, and precious little else. The boys went to one room and the girls to another. When it was mercifully over, the teacher sighed with relief. The class giggled uncontrollably, then huddled together during the next recess to find out what had happened in the opposite sex's room. My high school biology teacher, a dear man, couldn't say the word *sex* without blushing several shades of red. Mine wasn't a very systematic or thorough sex education. I don't remember any moral content at all. None. Zip. The church wasn't much help in that regard, either. It even managed to ignore the rather explicit sexuality of the Old Testament. David did what with Bathsheba? The Song of Solomon? Where's that?

Sexuality is a potent drive in our lives. If we fail to acknowledge its presence and energy, we risk being at its mercy. When we raise it to consciousness and discuss it with those we trust, it loses much of its power to cause feelings of guilt and shame. Sex is a normal part of life, sweet and beautiful and one of the deepest expressions of human love imaginable. Parents need to talk about its fundamental goodness with their children and teens, lest young people come to think of sex as cheap or dirty. Youth need to have their sexuality affirmed, to know deep down that their feelings are normal and healthy. Human sexuality is a gift from God, given to us in the beginning when we were created male and female.

It may not be a text originally intended to address our sexuality, yet it clearly speaks to the issue. I refer to Romans 8:1. "There is therefore now no condemnation for those who are in Christ Jesus." In our efforts to help youth safely navigate through the dangers of their first sexual activities, parents may be tempted to use scare tactics. Well-meaning though it be, avoid doing so. Don't make them fearful of their God-given drives and urges. Let there be no message of condemnation but rather share words of information and affirmation. I worry that some of those old horror stories, like telling them that certain behaviors will cause parts of their bodies to fall off, may still be told or at least implied.

The stakes are indeed high. Immature sexual actions can cause untold years of struggle and pain. But unloading a lifetime of guilt on a teen in an attempt to keep him or her chaste is seriously misguided. Over an extended period of time, parents cannot give youth the message that sex is bad, then expect them to discover its beauty and joy at the snap of a finger, at the very moment of marriage. The desired goals for expressing our sexuality should not be fear or guilt but respect for self and loving commitment to others.

Parents today have to deal with teenage sexuality far earlier and much longer than parents did in generations past. Consider these facts. In "olden times," say fifty to a hundred years ago, puberty occurred at ages fifteen to sixteen. Today it occurs closer to ages eleven to thirteen. Marriage used to happen on average at ages sixteen to eighteen. Now the average age is closer to twenty-three to twenty-four. The need for additional formal education and job training puts even more pressure on our youth. Their sexual drive begins earlier than ever, while at the same time they're asked to postpone longer the conditions appropriate for expressing it fully.

In addition, society's external controls have changed dramatically. The family used to be the strongest influence in young people's decision making. Today it's more likely to be their peers. Such as it was, sex information then was largely dispensed by the family, the church, and the school. These days the media, and television in particular, are the major vendors of this information. Once upon a time, almost all dating was chaperoned. Young couples were simply never alone together. Everywhere the young folks went, an adult was close by, watching and waiting. How things have changed! Today opportunities for privacy in dating are abundantly present, with both parents often working outside the home and the increase in single parenthood. Parents are spread too thinly to be everywhere or to see all, even if they wanted to. With the invention of the automobile and its availability to people of all ages, including youth, it's quite easy for young couples to be alone with each other for extended periods of time.

As parents, my wife and I have had to deal with these changing practices and values in some very concrete and practical ways, such as a son entertaining a young woman in his bedroom for hours upon hours. That might have been acceptable to us, except the door was shut. Tight. Maybe locked. And the lights were low. I could tell they were low from checking the tiny crack between the door and the carpet, not from peeking through the keyhole. So there! I was brought up to believe that if two young persons of the opposite sex were in the same bedroom, the door had better be wide open and the lights turned on bright. And there better be noise coming out of there, lots of it. Loud music or television didn't qualify. There had to be two people's voices speaking constantly and loud enough for parents to hear should they decide to listen. Total silence from the bedroom for more than a few moments would have meant Mom and/or Pop stopping by to offer a snack or to suggest we might like to continue our conversation in the living room, complete with a pesky little brother, two overly friendly cats, and one wiggly puppy.

In this matter of teenage sexuality, I have difficulty deciding which issues matter and which don't. Where should I bend my principles and where should I take a stand? I was taught, for example, that public displays of affection should be discreet. Things like holding hands, giving hugs, and putting an arm around the shoulder were permissible, in moderation, of course. Now on any trip to the mall, you're likely to see young couples with hands all over each other's bodies, in places I've always thought were appropriate to touch only in private, and in some cases only if persons were married. This may be a practice I'm going to have to accept. If I don't like it, too bad for me. I'll just have to look the other way.

Sexual mores have changed since I was a youth. I get daily and fairly graphic reminders of this fact. But there are ethical standards about sexuality that I'm not willing to yield to the pressures of contemporary society. I firmly believe that it's best for youth to refrain from the most intimate sexual practices until they've truly matured. To enter into a relationship of complete union with another person has the potential of being wonderful or of being disastrous. It can be a very loving moment or a very hurtful one. It depends on the maturity and wisdom of the persons involved, on their commitment and caring for each other. It must be more than a mere sexual coupling and it should move into an emotional, even a spiritual experience. Few if any youth are ready for such encounters.

I know how difficult it is for them to wait. I remember. So do most parents. It hasn't been that long since we felt the same desires and passions. But teenagers are simply not ready to accept the consequences of those actions. In addition, the very real threat today of contracting sexually transmitted diseases should serve as another deterrent. There are compelling reasons, at least from a parent's perspective, for youth to refrain from the more intense forms of sexual activity. Our ultimate aim is to get youth to agree with us.

We cannot expect to quickly resolve issues of sexuality that parents and teens have struggled with through the centuries, some probably since the dawning of human history. We can expect, however, to make progress by talking to one another about it, by sharing our ethical standards, by educating and informing them as much as possible. I leave you again with words of the apostle Paul, who wasn't exactly the Masters and Johnson of the first century. But he was a wise and learned man. " 'All things are lawful,' but not all things are beneficial. 'All things are lawful,' but not all things build up" (1 Cor. 10:23).

Teens can understand that simply because they have the physical ability or the power to do something, they don't necessarily have to act upon it. Curiosity, experimentation, and self-gratification are not adequate reasons for becoming fully sexually active as a teen. Their deepest, most profound expressions of sexuality can and should be postponed until they're ready to be a blessing to their partner, until they're truly capable of emotionally building each other up. Convincing them will not be easy. But try. Please try. Their future productivity and joy in life may well depend on your efforts.

10.
The Spiritual Care and Feeding of Teens

I was eighteen and off to college, a mixture of scared and excited. My freshman year was stressful but productive, except I don't remember once darkening the door of a church. I did attend church when I returned home for various holidays. My motive, though, was mostly to please my parents. I know they worried about my spiritual development, yet they seldom said anything. On one occasion my mother simply couldn't restrain herself. As I climbed on board the Greyhound bus after Christmas vacation, she blurted out, "You be sure to attend church, son!" I promised I would but my fingers and toes were all crossed. I also neglected to say when, having in mind somewhere around the year 2020.

What my parents didn't realize at the time was that they had given me a gift far more valuable than the habit of attending church. They gave me a solid start on a lifetime's spiritual journey. I apparently needed space to make my own decisions about being involved in the institution. It took three years, but by the last semester I was ready to make a renewed commitment to serve Christ through the church. Not only was I faithful in going to corporate worship, I heard and responded to the call of God to enter the ordained ministry.

I don't blame my parents for being concerned. I gave them ample cause. It may well have been their prayers that guided and sustained me through those times of doubting, questioning, and searching. I never lost sight of my spiritual quest. I learned early in childhood that my inner life is vitally important, that my faith journey would enrich and bless me forever.

I think it was during that same Christmas vacation when my mother sneaked a Bible into my school pack. Sitting alone on the long bus ride back to college, I grew increasingly lonely. Rummaging through my bag, I discovered her secret gift, a copy of the Letters of Paul translated by J. B. Phillips. Having no reading material other than boring college textbooks, I began reading my way through the various Epistles.

Imagine my surprise when the words of Scripture began to come alive for me. I particularly recall a verse in First John. "For loving God means obeying his commands, and these commands of his are not burdensome" (1 John 5:3 JBP). Not burdensome! I'd always felt that going to church was a chore; that keeping God's laws, most of which seemed negative to me, required duty of major league proportions. I'd always heard God's commands as an endless succession of oughts and shoulds, of can'ts and don'ts. From my point of view, religion might be important but it certainly wasn't much fun.

On that bus trip, my spiritual journey took a new direction and headed down the pathway leading to freedom and joy. My parents never knew what happened. I didn't tell them directly of my mini-conversion. I understand now that they surely knew of it. I didn't need to say a word. They could tell by my actions, by the happy look on my face, by my renewed enthusiasm for life. Getting me to attend church, while a worthy cause, didn't matter as much as encouraging my spiritual growth.

I believe this is true for parents and teens anytime, anywhere. Parents should offer them guidance in learning the different spiritual disciplines: meditation, prayer, Bible study, theological and ethical reflection, giving to the church and to other worthy charities. Above all else, strive to awaken their souls to spirituality. Take them by the hand and walk together through the beginning steps of their spiritual journeys. Tell them how precious life is. Reveal to them the sacred relationship we have to all other life. Help them sense the love of their Creator, which surrounds them constantly. Give them insights into the mystery and beauty of the universe. Teach them to be in tune with the divine music playing everywhere around them. Listen for them to resonate with the deepest purposes of life. And in everything, show them the way of thankfulness. If you make it through their entire spiritual sojourn and they have perfect attendance at Sunday school and worship, recite Mary's Magnificat while doing backflips. You have reason to say, "My soul magnifies the Lord, and my spirit rejoices in God my Savior" (Luke 1:47). Throw in a few psalms of praise for good measure.

Providing spiritual nurture for youth is much more than involving them in a variety of religious activities. Spirituality isn't really a matter of doing; it's a condition of being. While not ignoring the final destination, we need to focus more on the journey itself. The process of getting there isn't just half the fun. It's closer to 99 percent of it. I don't recommend dropping the kids off at the church door every Sunday morning, then heading back home to catch a football game on TV, or sipping coffee and eating donuts at a nearby restaurant. I suppose, of course, that it's preferable to their not ever being in church.

For this to be the truly wonderful, profound spiritual journey it can be, it must be shared. Parents and youth are intended to go on it together. We all benefit from having spiritual traveling companions, and our joy is increased when one of those partners is our own son or daughter. Then we all grow spiritually, young and old alike, each at his or her unique pace. Our goal as parents is to assist and guide youth toward spiritual maturity, helping them become the persons God created them to be. Our purpose is not to pry open reluctant youthful minds to cram inside an awareness of God. It's rather to awaken receptive young minds to the marvelous ways God is already present and at work in their lives.

A kind and compassionate parental manner is really the only way to accomplish this goal. If I'm correct, and I'm convinced I am, nagging them didn't work well when they were children. Oh, it might have gained temporary results, but it wasn't terribly effective over the long haul. It never is. Few, if any, persons have been pestered or scolded into the realm of God. Multitudes, however, have been hugged, loved, laughed, and gently led into it.

A healthy spirit issues from a relationship of total trust. It will be difficult for young persons to place their trust in a divine Parent when their earthly parents prove to be unreliable on a regular basis. Our spiritual lives are supposed to be as natural as putting on comfortable old slippers or wearing weather-beaten blue jeans, as common as brushing our teeth or washing our faces. Spirituality is to be woven into the very fabric of our daily lives.

Spiritual cloning may be a possibility but it certainly isn't a desirability. As parents, don't wrap up your theological answers in little boxes covered with pretty paper with cute bows on top. Sometimes the best gift you can give is to let them struggle with spiritual issues, thus helping youth develop the fruit of discernment. For young persons to learn the things of the inner life, simply hold in your hands the answers you've discovered over the years. Invite them to reach out and choose the ones they need.

You don't have to have all the answers to be a good spiritual director. In fact, just when you think you know it all is probably when you're least helpful. God gave teens minds for thinking, and spirits, too, with which to feel. Allow them to put both to fullest use. They're capable of having astounding spiritual insights and of making quite profound observations. You will be of most help to them when your own spiritual lives are in order. When parents nurture their souls, they'll have far more to offer their teens. Practice daily devotions if at all possible. Study the Scriptures, attend worship regularly, read thought-provoking books and articles, join a spiritual formation group.

Try parenting from your knees now and again. That is, pray frequently and earnestly. When teachers in ancient times were ready to share a great insight, they sat down while their audience stood around. When parents today need help, the best way to receive it is from their knees, from a position of openness and vulnerability. You will stand tallest before your teen after you have humbled yourself at the feet of your Creator.

In churches, preaching is usually a once-a-week event. In families with teenagers, that may be about once too often. When my own children were teens, I frequently got told, in no uncertain terms, to turn off my preacher voice. Apparently I'd forget where I was and crank up my voice from the diaphragm. "Hey, Pop," one of them would usually remind me, "this isn't the sanctuary and we aren't your congregation. This is the kitchen and we're just your kids. Take it easy."

Talk and visit with them as good friends, which they are and will always be. Keep monologues to a minimum. Carry on two-way conversations, dialogues with equal amounts of input from both sides. Encourage them. Prod, probe, and nudge them. Humor them when necessary. Stay abreast of their progress so you'll know when to take them off milk and put them on a diet of spiritual meat and potatoes. Don't be afraid to let them chew on some serious soul food.

Don't panic when you're stumped. Join the crowd. Simply say, "I don't know the answer, either." After all, you're not a panelist on a television quiz show. Spiritual growth is not like taking a true-false or multiple-choice test. It's a process of learning and living, of being open to new truths, of finding a more loving way of relating to others, of growing ever closer to God. There's a mystery at the heart of faith that we humans can never fathom. Youth don't expect you to be a great theologian or biblical scholar. A humble, honest, and loving parent is what they want and all that God expects.

None of us has to offer spiritual direction or nurture by ourselves. The greatest support system in the history of the world is available to every parent. It's called the church. While no denomination or congregation is perfect, the church is still the best resource we have for guidance in things of the Spirit. Its pews are filled with imperfect people. The hymns are often sung off-key. Sermons aren't always well-ordered, creative, and inspired. Yet the church is still a critically vital component in our journeys of faith. It provides the continuity of tradition, giving us a longitudinal perspective from the saints of some twenty centuries. It connects us to persons of all cultures, relating us to people of richly diverse educational backgrounds, socioeconomic levels, ethnic heritage, and age classifications. If offers a multitude of study, support, prayer, and fellowship groups.

Perhaps of highest importance, every moment of every day the church, the Body of Christ, lifts a steady stream of heartfelt prayers to God on behalf of families. These include prayers of forgiveness, petitions for peace and harmony in our homes, prayers for complete commitment between husbands and wives, and requests for loving relationships among all persons, including the larger families we call communities, states, and nations.

I still have my J. B. Phillips *Letters to Young Churches*. Nearly every page has underlinings with a rainbow effect from using different colored pens. It's worn and tattered and the front cover has come completely loose. But I don't care. Thirty-five years later I still love it and use it. It's one of my most prized possessions. If our house were to catch on fire, it's one of the first things I'd try to save.

11.
The Jolts and Joys of Parenting

*I*t happened the year he was fourteen. He was growing like a weed, eating like a horse, and getting stronger by the day. He couldn't pass a mirror, window, or other reflective surface without pausing to flex and admire his bulging biceps. Then he'd give a little wink and say, "Yes-s-s-s!"

It was a joy to watch our young man so pleased with his progress. He was an excellent athlete; played a tough, aggressive brand of junior high football; and was serious about lifting weights. He borrowed my old cast iron set, the one I'd gotten when I was in high school that now had rust around its edges. He pumped it religiously every evening for hours. You could hear the sounds of clanking metal reverberating throughout the house. He was able to bench-press considerably more than he weighed.

We should have seen what was coming next. Standing at full height before his mother, he challenged her to an arm-wrestling contest. She politely refused, but he kept pestering her. He just couldn't let it go. "What's the matter, Mom? Scared I'll beat you?"

"Not at all, dear," she answered. "I'm too busy." Actually, she *was* worried about losing and what consequences that might have on her authority with him. So she added, "What would your

friends think if I won? Wouldn't that be 1
embarrassment?"

"I'll take my chances," he replied confide

"Okay, young man, let's see what you'v ǝ
from the tone of her voice that she wasn't exactly sure about the
wisdom of doing this. But she was committed. The family
gathered close to watch the show. Friendly wagers were placed
on the outcome. I was about to bet on our son when I saw my
wife's eyes. She had that stubborn, determined, I-shall-prevail,
don't-mess-with-me look. I'd seen it before and knew what it
meant. I put my money on Mom.

Perched on kitchen stools, the contestants faced each other,
elbows together on the counter, right hands clasped. I served
as referee. "Three, two, one, go!" I yelled. Mom's arm didn't
budge an inch. The grin on our son's face evaporated and was
quickly replaced by a look of concern. He pulled. He grunted.
He began to breathe heavily. Little beads of perspiration
appeared on his forehead. Nothing happened. Then she made
her move. Slowly, inexorably, his arm started on a downward
arc toward the white countertop. In short order, his knuckles
scraped the surface.

"Hooray for Mom!" we all shouted. "You beat him!" He
couldn't believe it. An "old lady" who hadn't pumped a pound
of iron in her entire life had whipped him fair and square.

"That was a fluke," he complained. "I wasn't ready and I
didn't try very hard, either. I didn't want to hurt poor Mom. Let's
make it the best two out of three." Mom was agreeable. The
result of round two was exactly the same. As she raised her arms
in victory, our son quietly disappeared to his room. Soon the
unmistakable sounds of weights being lifted rose from the
basement.

Our teenage lad had made a slight miscalculation or two,
probably due to his youthful inexperience. He hadn't observed
the steely glint in his mother's eyes, and he did not understand
that strength is far more than muscles. It was a valuable lesson

for him, although at the time I don't think he fully appreciated it. He learned that the size of a person's heart counts for more than the bulk of his—or her—biceps. He also learned that moms are powerful people. Perhaps he hadn't noticed her carrying babies on her hip for entire mornings without relief. And maybe he didn't realize how much arm strength it takes to wash clothes, vacuum rugs, and mop floors. If you want to build up endurance, try lugging a squirming forty-pound toddler someplace he or she doesn't want to go. Courage of character will always win out over mere bodily strength.

Parents of teens are in special need of such inner power because they will be challenged again and again. Count on it. There's no cause to fret, however, if parents approach these tests not with dread but with good humor, expecting them to be exciting and memorable, anticipating a happy outcome. A positive attitude cannot transform every conflict. Some challenges are tough and demanding, and no amount of pleasant thinking will change that.

I'm convinced that if we expect teenagers to give us trouble, they'll try their hardest to live up to it. Conversely, if we expect them to bring us joy, they'll more than likely do exactly that. Of course, it's not quite that simple but there is some truth here. The challenges won't always be as funny as Mom's arm-wrestling episode. There'll be losses, too; probably many of them. But even then, we have reason to celebrate. I'm certain good old Mom would have found a way to be magnanimous in defeat and would have laughed all the way through it.

It was the apostle Paul who wrote, "Rejoice in the Lord always; again I will say, Rejoice" (Phil. 4:4). Goodness knows that Paul had more than enough trials and tribulations for one individual, yet he strongly urged people to be thankful, to offer praise, and to rejoice. Parents can be joyful not only when the going is easy and the way straight; not only when they're rested, have full tummies, and are feeling chipper, but always and everywhere. So you've got a cantankerous teenager? You say the month always lasts longer than your paycheck? Not only that but you've had a bad hair day because you couldn't get into the bathroom to fix it, because your teen spent hours preening? You have my compassion. Nevertheless, "Rejoice in the Lord always; again I will say, Rejoice"!

Listen once again to Paul, that wise letter writer of the first century. "Finally, beloved, whatever is true, whatever is honorable, whatever is just, whatever is pure, whatever is pleasing, whatever is commendable, if there is any excellence and if there is anything worthy of praise, think about these things" (Phil. 4:8). Focus on the wonderful, good qualities in young people. True, they no doubt make more than their share of mistakes. That's because they're still learning. Don't anticipate troubles and conflicts with them. Relax. Enjoy. The more problems you expect to have, the more you'll find. Be prepared for the difficulties. But don't go looking for them. Patiently and continually watch for sources of joy. Don't borrow trouble. The interest rate and terms are higher than you want to pay, and borrowed trouble is always compounded daily.

In family life there's simply no substitute for parents who truly, honestly enjoy teenagers. Teens need folks who like them just as they are, for who they are at that very moment. And there's lots about them to like. They're full of energy, eager to learn, ready to embrace new trends and novel ideas. Their humor is often fresh and off the wall. Their clumsiness has an appealing quality about it. You don't have to like teens in general, only the one or more who are chips off your own genetic block, and most of their friends as well.

When things at home don't quite work out the way they were planned; when problems occur and conflicts arise, today's parents tend to blame themselves. "What should we have done differently? Where did we go wrong?" Generations ago under similar circumstances, our parents asked, "What's that kid's problem? Whatever are we going to do with him or her?" The naïve confidence of parents but a few decades ago has been replaced by a pervasive anxiety. These days parents ask, "Are we doing a good job? Why didn't we do thus and such instead of this and that?" In addition, parents of children and teens receive conflicting advice from professionals and experts in the field. Put them on television talk shows and the muddled information may come in massive doses. No wonder parents are sometimes unsettled and confused.

Parents can no longer take solace in the stability of tradition. The traditional ways may have been right or wrong. Who knows? They were, however, comforting for parents. Parents then didn't feel so alone in their task. There was one basic, solid, and unchanging method of parenting. It gave them something to hold on to. It may have sometimes been restrictive, confining, and probably lacked creativity, but it did give parents a sense of security. They weren't wracked with doubts as to whether or not they were doing a good job.

The rules of the game have dramatically changed. Somebody moved the fences back—way back. Or they raised the baskets a couple of feet. These days parents don't simply wrestle with their arms. They now must tussle with global issues, moral values, and with spiritual powers. The struggles now engage a parent's whole body, mind, and soul. No wonder parents get weary.

The old securities are gone for parents, which may be for the better. But adequate new sources of family stability are not yet firmly in place. We've gone from "one right way" of parenting to "is there anybody in the world who has a clue?" We're living in a transitional period of history. It's both exciting and disturbing. We need to be patient with one another as we find our way through the maze. We'll make it. God has given us the intellectual resources and the will to do so. God has promised us the Holy Spirit, an Unseen Member of our families, our constant companion and guide.

It may be that we're asking the wrong question. Instead of wondering how to raise successful teenagers, perhaps we should be addressing the issue of how to be more effective parents. In other words, we need to pay attention to our own inner growth, strive to learn more about ourselves, take care of our physical bodies, and work hard on our spiritual development. As we become better, more mature persons, our parenting skills will certainly improve as well. We'll have more substance to offer our young people.

It's tempting, I know, for parents to take credit for their children's successes. When a youth does well, it's normal for Mom or Dad to puff up with pride, step forward, and say, "That's my kid!" Being proud of her or him is natural and good. Taking all the credit isn't. Let your teenager bask in the limelight, stand in the glow, and enjoy the accolades. You may have done a lot behind the scenes to make it all possible. Bravo! You deserve to feel warm and happy all over. Pat yourself on the back. But remember, your kid is the one who actually did it. So get in line and offer your congratulations as well.

When parents take major credit for young persons' achievements, they may also feel as though they must shoulder the blame when those same young persons fail. The parent-child relationship isn't that simple. We're not dealing with an algebraic equation where if x = 5, then 3x = 15. Family life does not have mathematical certainty. There are complex genetic, cultural, social, educational, emotional, and spiritual factors for which to account. And at some point in their growth, youth themselves must accept responsibility for their own choices, attitudes, beliefs, and the direction their lives are going.

Parenting teens includes the fullest possible range of experiences and human emotions. There'll be challenges and affirmations, hurts and humor, problems and praise, thrilling highs and depressing lows, jolts and joys. Through them all, strive for steadiness. All too quickly, "This too shall pass." They'll be off on their own adventures and explorations, and you'll be left with your memories. Make them sweet and lovely ones. And while you're at it, may I suggest you not challenge your mom, no matter what her size or age, to an arm-wrestling contest. Save your strength for loving your teenager. You'll likely need it!

12.
Your Labor Is Not in Vain

*Y*ou know the old saying, "You can lead a horse to water, but you can't make it drink." The same is true of teenagers. You can lead your young persons to wonderful opportunities and present them with possibilities galore. You may suggest, direct, urge, and plead. But you cannot force them to take advantage of any of it. If they choose to drink of your offerings, they will. And if they don't; well, "you can lead a horse to water, but . . ." They must decide to bend down and take that first sip. They must hold their own cup and place themselves under the waterfall of God's grace.

Parents are called to give their children as much love as they possibly can, to do the very best they know how. For their part, youth are called to receive, accept, and follow as best they are able. No matter how many times teens refuse to listen or respond favorably; no matter how many times you lead them to water and they will not drink, you as a parent must continue trying. You are to patiently show them where to find the sources of clean, pure, and wholesome life.

Keep putting fresh water in the trough. One day the horse may make the connection between its thirst and drinking the water. Some day, teenagers will understand and make the association between parents' advice and their desire to experience life fully. It may happen soon or it may take years. But their thirst for knowledge will eventually cause them to appreciate the wisdom of their parents. They will finally want to draw from your parental well containing spiritual power and emotional stability. Constantly fill that container with life-giving water because when they finally do drink from it, you don't want its contents to be stale, stagnant, or muddy. You want your young person refreshed by its sweetness and blessed by its purity.

Hang in there. Keep making the offer. Remember: "This too shall pass." Their respect and receptivity toward you will change for the better. First Corinthians 15:58 would make an excellent text for parents of teens to put on their refrigerators or carry in their pockets. "Therefore, my beloved, be steadfast, immovable, always excelling in the work of the Lord, because you know that in the Lord your labor is not in vain."

Parents aren't likely to receive frequent affirmation from various family members. In fact, they may well get the opposite: complaints, criticism, objections, and a wide variety of other protests. Most parents have heard them all.

"You never let me have any fun."

"You can't tell me who my friends can be."

"I'm the only kid in the entire school who never gets to go to R-rated movies."

"Everybody else my age gets to stay out as long as they want."

"I'm old enough that I don't need you telling me what to do."

"If you really loved me, you'd let me go to the party."

"It's my money. I'll spend it however I want!"

It can be a lengthy litany, played out as dependable as a train schedule or the TV guide.

Parents, of course, need to consider the possibility that youth's complaints contain kernels of truth, though it usually comes with so much chaff it can be difficult to find. But make the effort. Sort through the fluff to discover the basic idea or their true feelings. It's also quite possible that your daughter or son is overreacting to a momentary disappointment. When that's the case, they simply need recovery time for their minds to settle and their spirits to calm. I suggest backing away to provide them room. If at all possible, avoid confrontation. Use it only as a last resort. You may gain a conflict-free victory by doing nothing. Think about it. What does it gain a parent to win the argument but in the process lose a young person's affection?

When the threat of rebellion lurks on the horizon; when you're feeling like an ineffective or even a terrible parent; when you're insecure about the kind of job you're doing, how do you pull yourself through? How do you get it back together again? Don't count on positive feedback from the family troops. You may get some. If so, cherish it. Store it in your heart to draw from when the going gets tough again.

How do you as a parent calm your nerves when you're confused and don't have the faintest idea what to do next? It's not easy wondering if all your labor is in vain, if you're IN the way rather than ON the way with them. There are no magic answers in parenting. It's a matter of good common sense, the power of positive thinking, and lots of prayer.

First, take a giant step back and look at the big picture. At any given moment, in the heat of battle, things may appear rather bleak. Review your Seven-Year Plan of raising teenagers. What's that you say? It's the hopes and dreams you have for that headstrong youth of yours, that one day he or she will be a mature young adult, a person who has grown intellectually and emotionally by leaps and bounds, who is well on the way to being a productive citizen. Short-term goals are important but never enough by themselves. They do serve a purpose: getting you through each day. But life is so much more than surviving until evening in order to fall back into the same rumpled bed you crawled out of a few hours earlier.

Parents must be capable of rising above the fray lest they become completely entangled in the stresses and hassles of daily duty. If we're too close, we tend not to see the progress they're making. We can miss their growth since it occurs slowly. Surely you know what friends or family say when they see your son or daughter after a considerable lapse of time. "My goodness!" they exclaim. "You've grown like a weed! I do believe you're taller than your parents. What are they feeding you?" They notice the development because they're looking from a distance, because they have a larger perspective. Parents ought to stay close to their teenagers, yet every so often they need to move aside and take a clear and objective look.

This includes refraining from making hard-and-fast parental assumptions about teens on the basis of one day's experience, or a week's, a month's, or any other limited length of time. Anyone can have a bad day. I admit to having months that are unproductive, when I'm totally out of sorts. It's quite possible for people of all ages to undergo years in which they're just out of sync with life. Therefore, a historical perspective in rearing teens is helpful. Glance backward. Remember the kind, sweet child this tall, awkward person used to be. Make mental notes of where there has been progress and where there hasn't. It will give you valuable insights into his or her current behavior. Then look ahead and reflect on the potential this special person has and meditate on the dreams you hold in your heart. Wondering won't provide any concrete answers, but it will offer clues and give you tantalizing hints of their future. It also will energize and inspire you for the long and demanding trip ahead.

Second, talk to parents who have gone this way before and lived to tell about it. There are usually quite a few who are happy to oblige. Listen to them when they share the mystery of how their teenagers grew to become decent human beings and responsible young adults. You may well be encouraged and determined to "go thou, and do likewise." Experienced parents of young persons can alert those beginning the trip to the pitfalls, potholes, twists, and turns in the road ahead. You as a parent are at least as loving as they are and probably a great deal smarter. If they made it, so can you.

Permit me a friendly word of caution. Don't accept as gospel every word spoken by those who have been through the parental wars and have the scars to prove it. They don't mean to exaggerate. They can't help it. It comes as naturally to them as it does to those who tell fish stories. Parents who have successfully completed the course and have received their diplomas will often take literary license when telling of their exploits. It seems the further removed they get from the original experience, the more they embroider the facts. I should know. I'm very good at it myself.

Third, stubbornness is a quality found abundantly in mules and in parents of teenagers. It can be quite useful when one knows how to control and direct it. At its worst, it can exasperate young people, who interpret it as uncaring and unresponsive. At its highest expression, we call it faithfulness or commitment. The interpretation may depend on which side of the issue you're standing. Parenting might be considered a long-term investment in young persons' lives. As such, don't second-guess your original decisions. You made them, now find the courage to fulfill them. If the kids think you're being a stubborn old jackass, so be it. Wear it as a badge of honor.

In the fable of the tortoise and the hare, the tortoise must surely have been a parent. He trudged along unmindful of the distance, tired and slow of foot, but determined and undeterred by obstacles on his way to the finish line. In the job description of parenting, this same kind of plodding faithfulness is far more valuable than a flashy outward style. Sparkle is quickly gone and glitter soon scattered. Faithfulness is an abiding quality, a lifetime venture.

Fourth and finally, don't be swayed too much by the words of youth. They may not intentionally try to mislead you. They simply do not always know their own minds. They may not be capable of counting the total cost of what they promise. Consequently, pay greater attention to their deeds. Actions have an eloquence that mere words can never attain. Jesus once told a delightful and very human parable about a parent who had two sons. You may read it in its entirety in Matthew 21:28-32. The father asked son number one to go work in the orchard. "No can do, Pop. I'm too busy playing around." But later, the boy had a change of heart, rolled up his sleeves, and did the job. Then old Dad asked son number two the very same thing.

"Sure thing, Pop. I'll get to it right away." But he never did. I'm sure he meant to. It was just never quite convenient for him.

"Now," asked Jesus, "which of these young men was obedient to his father?" The crowd of listeners replied that it was the lad who actually went out and did the work. In the same manner, we should take seriously the words of youth. Even more we need to observe their actions. The proof of the pie isn't in the recipe; it's not in the numbers and words written on a card. They're helpful. But it's in the eating, in the taste, particularly when it's blackberry pie warm from the oven and has a large scoop of vanilla ice cream on top.

"Your labor is not in vain." Our labor as parents may sometimes be long, hard, and painful. Single parents have it particularly rough. There's no other adult in the house to bounce ideas off of, with whom to compare parenting notes, to console you when you've totally blown it, or to share your burdens. Parenting may often include all-night vigils, tired feet from pacing the floor, and knees stiff from praying. There will be blisters and sore muscles from the effort of trying to keep pace with the demands of parenting. But the labor performed by parents does count for something. It counts for a great deal! In fact, I believe that the work of parenting has eternal consequences. This statement is not intended to put additional pressure on parents but to remind them that theirs is a significant ministry, an incredibly important and irreplaceable labor of love.

So always keep fresh water in that trough. You never know when they'll be ready to drink from it.

13.
When the Best Answer Is to Listen

Once upon a time there was a family in which no one ever got to finish a sentence. One member would start to express a thought, and another, without fail, would complete it. Their conversations needed only commas, semicolons, and dashes, never periods—at least not until the close of day when the last one to bed said, "Good-night." They really didn't intend to be rude. They just didn't know how to listen. It may have been a genetic problem. When their mouths opened, apparently their ears automatically went shut. A typical dialogue in their household sounded like this:

"It's my turn to watch . . ."

"Seinfeld? You always get to watch whatever . . ."

"Do not! I don't ever get to . . ."

"Mom, tell John it's my turn to . . ."

"Now, Aimee, calm down, you . . ."

"Hey, who ate the donut I was . . ."

"You didn't put your name on it, so how was I . . ."

"I hate reruns of *I Love* . . ."

"*Lucy* was a better show than . . ."

"Say, you never paid me back that dollar . . ."

"I don't remember you lending me a . . ."

"It was at lunch, Monday, and you didn't have . . ."

"Turn it back right now to channel . . ."

"Mom, John's being a . . ."

You get the point. They never learned to listen. And they were none too polite about it, either.

Listening is a gift, a very precious one that is in short supply. That is unfortunate because it is a gift we need. All people yearn to be heard, to have someone listen to their deepest thoughts and feelings. It is a gift each one of us can offer. True listening is a healing experience. Through it we know we've been heard, accepted, and valued by another person. In a crisis, it brings us comfort; when making a decision, it offers wisdom; when in turmoil, it helps us clarify; when in pain, it brings us healing.

We also need opportunities to share our everyday experiences. It helps us find our way through the stress and grind of daily life. It enables us to integrate the numerous disconnected events with which we must cope. A good listener assists us in the work of connecting our thoughts with our feelings and of becoming whole persons. When sorrow enters our lives, it is indeed comforting to have someone who will listen to our pain. When we experience a success and are bubbling over with joy, it's wonderful to find a listener who will share in our happiness. Romans 12:15 puts it succinctly: "Rejoice with those who rejoice, weep with those who weep."

It takes a significant amount of time to be a good listener. Perhaps that's part of our problem in these busy, sometimes hectic days. Our attention spans are entirely too short. To listen, you have to hold still, relax, and yet remain alert. Parents can use listening to great advantage. It's a thousand times more effective than nagging to draw out the inner feelings of a teenager. It's a gentle and kindly method. It communicates caring for the other person. When you actively, creatively listen, you tell them that you value their opinions and ideas. Their views have worth for you, enough to invest yourself and your time in them. Listening to young persons can help them sustain the struggle to find their identity. It assists them in considering their available options and making wise decisions regarding their future.

One of the wonderful qualities of listening is its nondirective nature. That is, it leaves the decision-making responsibility, the burden of proof, with the speaker. Parents who are accomplished listeners help teens reach their own conclusions. Listening to youth doesn't provide them with easy answers or let them off the hook. The young person is still accountable for his or her judgments and actions. If you tell another person what to do, if you hand out lots of advice, you may remove that person's need to struggle for answers. When we must work hard mentally to find solutions, it strengthens our minds for future and perhaps bigger decisions. Our motivation to succeed is enhanced. When we claim ownership in a decision and have a personal stake in it, we want to see a satisfactory conclusion and are more likely to give ourselves wholeheartedly to the task.

Many parents probably err in wanting to tell teens too much, in giving too many directions and overwhelming them with suggestions, in literally inundating them with instructions and orders. Youth do need guidance; a great deal of it. But an indirect delivery system such as listening often works best. That's because youth need plenty of room for making their own decisions, including the very real possibility of making messes, spills, and mistakes of every imaginable variety. We want to protect them from the dead ends and disasters we as parents discovered from our years of experience. It's an understandable desire. But it may rob them of one very essential ingredient, their own personal involvement, which stimulates their intellectual and emotional maturation.

Teens don't always need answers. In fact, they may benefit far more from a parent who quietly but intently listens; one who acts as their mentor and confidant, as a silent and supportive companion on their journey. This kind of listening is not indifferent or passive. It's very intentional and active. If you simply sit there like a bump on a log, it won't work. The TV has got to be turned off, the newspaper put down. Halftime during the football game won't cut it. They won't feel that what they have to say is important to you if your focus is on something or someone else. Make and keep eye contact. Provide them with nonverbal feedback: a smile, a frown, a nod, a raised eyebrow—whatever is appropriate and natural.

When you respond with words, try to be brief. No half-hour sermons, please. Summarize what you think you've heard them say to make certain you're hearing not only their words but their meaning. Go beyond their language and be sensitive to what they're feeling in their hearts. Just as we can read between the lines of a book, parents can listen between the sentences teens speak. Sometimes what they don't say, those moments of silence, can be as profoundly significant as what they do verbalize.

I suggest practicing the art of listening. It doesn't seem to be intuitively learned by most folks. And even if it comes easily to you, there's always room for improvement. Once in a while, turn off every noise-making appliance in your house. Sit in silence, shut your eyes, and listen. Or go outside early in the morning before your town or city comes to life, and listen for the sounds of the world around you, for the rustle of trees in the wind, for the cheerful songs of birds as they greet the dawn. I find pleasure in listening to the sounds of our community awakening and beginning to bustle about.

Do not be judgmental in your listening. Freely receive whatever is said. Do not say to yourself, "That's important and that's not." Simply listen. Those teenage concerns that seem minor to you may, in fact, be of major importance to them. And how they feel is what counts. Their concerns may be at the bottom of your personal totem pole. But if it's important to them, as you listen it will become important to you as well. A blemish here, a stray hair there, a missed phone call, not having a popular brand of clothing, these may not seem like much to you. But any one of these could feel like the end of the world to them. Hear what they're saying on their own terms and not according to your values and expectations.

Listening is a demanding, exacting discipline, one which society today does little to help or encourage us to develop. We're surrounded by noise, much of it loud and intrusive. We face such a multitude of concerns in our lives as parents, such an overwhelming amount of tragedies in the larger world, that we're tempted to shut out every other request for help. At the very least, we're so distracted that a teenager's solitary voice may be ignored or lost in the commotion.

Listening is tough enough when we're rested and feeling good about ourselves. When we're tired and down in the dumps, it can be a challenge of monumental proportions. A young person's need to talk and be heard won't necessarily correspond to our parental mood swings. You can count on their wanting you to listen to their pain and troubles at precisely the most demanding time in your own life. Thankfully, it works the other way around, too. I recall occasions when my chin was scraping the pavement and my children would tell me of a joyful event in their lives. They buoyed my sagging spirit with their enthusiasm, until by the time they'd finished with their happy story, I was my old chipper self again.

Genuine caring, and sincere listening recognizes the truth that some problems are not quickly resolved. While many questions are answered relatively easily, others defy solutions. Some problems simply have no answers. Nothing you as a parent can say or do will solve it. Listening may be the only alternative. It will not solve the dilemma or erase the hurt, but it will give your teenager the power, the courage, and the will to live with it, to have the strength to make the best of difficult situations. Listening to youth may be the parental equivalent of kissing the "ouchies" of small children.

Having someone truly listen to us is very affirming. In our humanness, we sometimes feel as though our ideas are stupid, our questions are the dumbest ones anybody ever asked, that our feelings are out of sync with everybody else's. When our fears and anxieties are heard and accepted by one other member of the human race, we experience feelings of solidarity with the whole lump. It's like leaven for us. We no longer feel so alone and isolated. We rise from our beds to greet the morning sun. We go forth to meet the day with renewed confidence. We feel loved, all because someone listened to us. It is indeed a great gift!

Another name for God might well be the Eternal Listener. Even before we speak a word, before we form it on our lips, God hears it. At its highest level, prayer is listening. It's a divine-human interaction in which we're attentive to God and God bends close to hear our pleas. Jesus was a marvelous listener, no doubt the best of all time. He sat at the feet of great rabbis in the Temple, soaking up their teaching. He heard the cries of the woman at the well in Samaria, the lament of the lame man at the Pool of Bethesda, the sorrow and grief of Mary and Martha at the death of their brother Lazarus. He heard the plaintive request of the woman who silently touched the hem of his garment. He listened in agony while praying in the garden of Gethsemane, as he uttered those famous words, "Not my will, but thine be done." Then he waited and listened in order to discern God's will.

Both parents and teenagers have Someone who faithfully hears them every minute of every day. When you need to do so, you may confidently pour out the thoughts in your mind and the feelings of your heart before God. You will be gladly, freely received and fully heard at any hour of the day or night, no matter how close or far away you may be. We who are created in the image of God possess that same godly gift of listening. Use it frequently; share it generously. Don't wait for another to ask you to listen. Offer it immediately, spontaneously, and graciously.

Those who are good listeners will be among the most blessed of souls in this life, and I am quite certain in the next life as well.

14.
How's Your Parental Balance?

*D*o you as a parent ever feel like one of those stage performers who try to balance a bunch of plates—breakable ones at that—on the tips of skinny poles? The key to success seems to be giving each plate a good, hard spin. If it keeps rotating fast enough, the balance is maintained. But if the performer gets too many plates going at the same time, disaster is soon to follow. The entertainer runs frantically hither and yon, but to no avail. He or she simply cannot give each plate enough momentum, and it inevitably gets the wobbles. Plates begin crashing to the floor, shattering into hundreds of pieces. At that point, no amount of effort can save the situation.

So it is with parents in general and with those who have teens in particular. This is a task for somebody who is skilled enough and fully equipped to serve as the director of a three-ring circus, or as a juggler who can keep a dozen balls in the air at the same time. Parenting teens is a demanding job requiring considerable powers of concentration, high levels of energy, and a pleasant temperament with ductile properties. This last quality refers to the ability to be stretched thin, to be pulled and tugged simultaneously from several sides, to be forceably hammered out or pounded flat. Sounds like a normal day in the life of a family with teenagers, doesn't it? Parents need the capacity to snap back rapidly into emotional shape rather than to snap in frustration at others. A ductile metal can be extended to its limit and twisted into a pretzel shape yet not break, a highly desirable characteristic for parents of teenagers as well.

If you've got young people around the house and under your feet, perhaps literally, balance is a prerequisite for survival and/or success. I wonder sometimes why there aren't more courses for expectant parents of teens. When a baby is anticipated, parents go to classes to learn how to breathe deeply, how to relax, and how to enjoy the experience in spite of the pain. Well, birthing a teenager can be difficult, too. When a child turns twelve, parents should enroll in a support group, practice sighing loudly and often, perfect the motion of removing money from a billfold, and learn how to pace the bedroom floor late at night. It might also be helpful for them to practice doing flips on one of those gymnastic balance beams.

Once your children become teens, there'll be a thousand and one activities, programs, details, and duties to be managed, and that's just before lunch. There are school conferences to attend; emergency deliveries of the books, papers, and lunch money they forgot; and another trip to the gas station because teens frequently mistake the family car for a taxi. You've got to take them to music lessons and soccer practice. In spite of all these demands, they still expect you to get them there on time and be early to pick them up. You must go shopping for food even though you spent a bundle on groceries just yesterday. Food disappears faster from your refrigerator than a jet airplane flying into a fog bank, more quickly from your cupboards than light disappearing into a black hole. You may be asked to take them to the library on an errand of mercy, helping to research a five-page term paper due at 8:00 the next morning. Then it's back to the grocery store for the laundry soap you forgot. You can't do the wash without it and they simply can't be seen in public unless their favorite outfit is clean and ready to wear. After a quick visit to your drive-through bank to make a deposit to cover your last grocery check, it's home to cook dinner; except you forgot the ground beef and you promised them meat loaf. So it's trip number three that day to see your friendly grocer. The person at the checkout counter gives you a compassionate smile, which helps calm your jangled nerves. Need I go on?

Coordinating the family's activities while keeping your parental balance is no small miracle. It's a dizzying schedule to maintain. And somewhere in all of that, you're supposed to squeeze in time for yourself. I have only one thing to say about that: "Hah!" Make that two things: "Hah-hah!"

The preacher in the Old Testament book of Ecclesiastes understood the principle of balance and perspective. "For everything there is a season," he wrote, "and a time for every matter under heaven: a time to be born, and a time to die; a time to plant, and a time to pluck up what is planted; . . . a time to weep, and a time to laugh; a time to mourn, and a time to dance; . . . a time to seek, and a time to lose; a time to keep, and a time to throw away; . . . a time to keep silence, and a time to speak" (Eccles. 3:1-2, 4, 6, 7*b*).

Loosely paraphrasing this text for parents' benefit, we might add, "There's a time to bring children into this world, and a time to send them out into the world; a time to teach them, and a time to let them learn on their own; a time to serve and wait upon their needs, and a time to take care of our own needs; a time to work hard for them, and a time to rest and pray; a time to give answers, and a time to ask questions; a time to protect them from errors, and a time to let them make their own mistakes."

The pressures and demands of parenting teens can bump our personal lives off-center and make us unbalanced. We don't intend it to happen. We just become so involved in their activities and so concerned about their problems that we tend to forget our own needs as human beings. Parents do have rights, although some days they'd be hard pressed to name even one. They are real persons complete with real concerns, insecurities, hopes and plans, and a whole range of other normal feelings. It's not selfish of parents to spend time focusing on their own affairs and inner leadings. In the long run it benefits the entire family. When parents nurture themselves and honor their own basic human requirements, they are better able to maintain a high level of energy and keep a positive attitude.

Parents of adolescents have varied and complex duties to harmonize. They must delicately balance a teen's need for increasing freedom with their parental desire to maintain a semblance of control. We might think of this issue as being a continuum with a line starting at birth and reaching to young adulthood. Complete dependence is on the far left side of the page, total independence on the right. At its best, the maturation process moves gradually and smoothly across the line. In normal family life, however, the best scenario is often a fiction found only in our wildest dreams. It's what families on television sitcoms miraculously achieve one minute before the final commercial. Back in reality, we often bounce and tumble along as best we can. Oftentimes progress is slow, occasionally fast, and sometimes in spite of our efforts it seems as though we're sliding backward.

Teens push for greater freedom. Parents lobby for greater accountability. The continuum may at times appear to be a train track where two locomotives are speeding directly toward each other. Obviously, this is not a desirable condition. Collisions and other unpleasantries result. The image families seek is one in which parents and youth move peacefully together toward the young person's developing independence. It will seldom happen the way an arrow zings toward the target, straight and true. It will move up and down, back and forth, and zigzag for good measure. Don't worry overly much about these minor fluctuations. Just make certain that overall you and your teen proceed in the same general direction.

It helps parents preserve their equilibrium when youngsters in the family maintain a relatively even keel. And it helps youth proceed ahead confidently when their parents are fairly well squared away. This happy state of euphoria doesn't usually last long. A best friend moves away. A grandparent becomes seriously ill. A favorite pet dies. Mother or Father gets laid off from work. The young person has a fender bender in the school parking lot. Fortunately, inner balance is not dependent on outward peace and tranquillity. We can experience turmoil and upset yet find calmness within that sustains us through the trouble.

Psalm 46 is a passage I embrace when my world feels as though it's coming apart. "God is our refuge and strength, a very present help in trouble. Therefore we will not fear, though the earth should change, though the mountains shake in the heart of the sea; though its waters roar and foam, though the mountains tremble with its tumult" (Ps. 46:1-3). The psalmist reminds us that God's support is always present when circumstances around us spin out of control. The Creator helps us keep our balance and remain upright through them all.

Balancing the demands of time is one of the most frustrating pressures parents must face. It's one of those tensions that never quite goes away. It defies a permanent solution. You simply have to deal with it day after difficult day. How well I remember the struggle to balance the hours I worked outside the home with those I spent inside our home with family. Just when I thought I'd gotten these two participants in the time game playing as a team, one or both would ask to have the contract renegotiated. There'd be a change at the office—a rush order might come in, or somebody on the staff became ill. Whatever the cause, the end result always meant longer hours at work. As if that weren't enough, it added greater mental and emotional stress as well, which then translated into less energy when I finally did arrive home.

Try as I might, sometimes I couldn't avoid bringing pieces of work home. Frequently they were rather large chunks. If they weren't stuffed in my briefcase, they rattled around in my brain or made grumbling sounds in my stomach. I resented their hitching a ride home with me. But I couldn't always convince them to stay at the office where they belonged.

Of course, the reverse is also true. A teenage daughter may have a crisis in a relationship and need to talk it through, perhaps at length. A school program features your teen as a soloist. The church's youth group goes on a retreat and cannot find anybody but you to chaperone it. Or the Christmas holiday season arrives and several million preparations have to be done in addition to your regular hectic schedule. At such times, your work may suffer.

Then there's getting ready for those famous family birthday parties. That one special gift, the one she or he simply has to have, cannot be found anywhere in town. Someone, in my case good old Dad, is elected to check every discount store, mall, downtown business, and mom-and-pop operation in the entire area. This takes time, energy, and half a tank of gas. Time spent doing one task is time not available for another. It's simple mathematics.

There may be moments, days, even months, when it feels as though work and home are ganging up on you. "I need you at home," says your family. "No, we need you more," insists your employer or business. Since there's only one of you, you have to make a stressful choice. You're precariously perched between two irresistible forces. You can try to satisfy both by giving up eating, sleeping, and all bathroom privileges. But sacrificing your physical health on the altar of parental duty is not wise. Everybody, especially you, loses. There probably aren't any completely satisfactory solutions. But there must be a better way than being pulled, tugged, drawn and quartered by competing loyalties.

There is. Parents of teenagers need to devise a system of time management that works for them. The "squeaky wheel" method is frequently used but is not effective. Running from one crisis to another is tiring business and never allows you to address the root causes of the problem. The "back burner" system can be employed as long as you understand it's a temporary solution. Even on low heat, you'll eventually boil over and make a puddle on the stove top.

Busy parents can try bargaining with the Eternal One for an additional allotment of time. If a thousand years are as one day to God, you'd think it would be fairly simple for him to add a few hours to each day. It would be great, for example, if Wednesday had twenty-eight hours. God could do it if God really wanted to. Apparently, nobody's made the Almighty an offer in this matter he couldn't refuse.

Attempting to manage one's time is a better course of action. Don't fritter it away, at least not often. If you're going to waste time, do it well. Be creative. Do not ever "kill time." It's far too precious to dispatch like that. If you have no use for it, give it to somebody else. Or share some with your family. Spend it in prayer.

Learn how to say "No!" and make it stick. Concentrate your energies on people and projects where you can make a difference. Channel your time and talents. Don't let them run all over the place. Keep your focus. Make a "to do" list and include several whimsical items.

- Lunch with the boss
- Mow the lawn
- Gas in the car
- Go for a walk with daughter
- Pick up suit at cleaners
- Buy a rosebud for spouse
- Go to the bank
- Find the basketball and play a game of H-O-R-S-E with son and his buddies
- Let them win (as if there was a choice)

Program time for caring and loving into the very fabric of your daily routine. Don't give only leftover moments to the people for whom you care the most. Subscribe to the "Don't bite off more than you can chew" branch of time management. When no one is looking, talk sternly to your watch, clocks, and calendars. Remind them who is in charge.

The main thing about parenting is to remember the main thing. Love those kids! Keep moving ahead in the direction of caring and serving them. When you're riding a bicycle, if you stop or slow down too much, you'll likely topple over. But if you maintain your forward progress, your balance will take care of itself. Parenting teenagers is somewhat similar. Even when you're uncertain of precisely how to proceed, keep pedaling. It's easier to turn a bike around and change direction than to scrape yourself off the pavement.

Finally, in the struggle to manage your time, persevere. Now and then time may graciously yield to you. More often than not it will fight you every step of the way. Do not be dissuaded; be strong; keep the faith. Have hope because eventually, "This too shall pass." Sooner than you may think, you'll have on your comfy slippers with a blanket wrapped around your arthritic shoulders, a fire will be crackling in the stove, and you'll be sitting there rocking back and forth. You and time will have made your peace. You may even have extra time on your hands, so much it'll run down into your lap. It could happen.

In the meantime, spread your arms wide, put one foot in front of the other, and balance as best as you are able. Glance ahead for trusted friends when you may need a bit of steadying. It's quite all right to lean on others. They won't mind at all. In fact, it will make them feel useful.

15.
Keep Open the Door of Your Heart

I've heard parents of teens say with absolute certainty, with no wavering to their voices at all, "Once they leave home, they're gone for good. We'll never let them move back. They're on their own, and that's that!" Jokes are told about parents who threaten to change the locks on their doors so their grown-up offspring can't get in; who laugh about moving into a small apartment so other family members won't have room to live with them; who chuckle about leaving no forwarding address or getting an unlisted phone number. Personally, I'm not amused. Of course, I don't think mother-in-law jokes are very funny, either. I had a wonderful second mother. We've been blessed by good children; not perfect, but solid, quality kids. They know the welcome mat is always out. We thoroughly enjoy their visits. They also know that if they are in trouble and need a place of security, a place to heal, a hot shower or a square meal, our door will be open wide.

I'm not saying we'd let them run back home to avoid dealing with a minor conflict, to flee to dear sweet Mom and Dad at the first sign of difficulty in a marriage, or to give college a half-hearted try and then escape responsibility by hiding in their old room. Not at all. We expect them to be mature and handle their problems with perseverance and wisdom. We've learned, however, that when it comes to parenting, never say never. Things happen that none of us can predict. Both their and our best laid plans may not come to pass. Sometimes we have so many detours on the road of life that the alternate route becomes the main thoroughfare. At such stressful moments, a brief stay in their original nest may be quite acceptable, even desirable.

One of our adult daughters came home to live for more than a year. She needed a safe haven, which we gladly provided. When she was a young teen, she was the one who slammed doors, perfecting the art through frequent practice. She wasn't a large person but she could rattle the whole house with one of her special slams. No matter how many times she slammed, we tried to keep our hearts open to her, not to slam a parental door in response. We had to do some serious talking to make it work. But we did. Her return home proved to be a marvelous blessing for all three of us. We got to know and appreciate one another in new ways. Even without asking my spouse for her opinion, I know we'd do it again in a second.

Frankly, I don't understand how a parent can make such definite and final pronouncements as "When you turn eighteen, kid, you better hit the road. Don't come crawling back the first time you run out of money." It makes me wonder about the quality of the relationship they had all those years when their son or daughter was at home. My theory is "Once a parent, forever a parent." Yes, the day-to-day responsibilities are substantially lessened. The financial obligations are modified. Even though they establish their own households, they will always be your children. And you will never cease being their parent. The relationship changes; the bond of love remains.

It's possible to take exception to the lifestyles and value systems of teenagers, yet to love them fully and unconditionally. You don't have to agree on everything in order to care about them. One of our sons and I went through a prolonged period when we were on opposite sides of the planet. If he was day, I was night. If he was summer, I was winter. I loved that boy dearly. Still do, although he is now a man. We had more than our share of "in your face" confrontations. He and I verbally sparred for who knows how many rounds. We simply didn't look at life the same. We lived under the same roof, put our pants on one leg at a time, and both have blue eyes, but that's where the similarities pretty much stopped. He was a teenage political conservative. I was a middle-aged liberal. Still am. He's a fighter/scrapper. I'm a peace lover/pacifist. He likes guns, hunting deer, fishing for trout, motorcycles, and fast boats. I like a good book, a cup of piping hot tea, pruning rose gardens, and playing the violin. He didn't know the difference between a spatula and an egg beater. I'm no gourmet cook, but I enjoy puttering around in the kitchen. He didn't have much use for the institutional church. I was deeply committed to it and very involved.

Nevertheless, we now respect each other a great deal. I admire the way he sticks to his beliefs and convictions. I'm proud of his honesty, his sense of humor, and his dependability. He is hard-working, caring, dedicated to helping society improve, and loves his family with all his heart. What more could I, his parent, ask? So he's a Republican, likes country-western music, and listens to Rush Limbaugh. I'm not, don't, and wouldn't ever. What's the difference? These are personal decisions. As long as we're true to ourselves, we shall both honor that.

I believe this is what it means to be a consistent parent. We may waffle on our discipline, renege on a promise or two, be too lenient one day and too strict the next. That's part of what being human is all about. By far the most important demonstration of parental consistency is to constantly accept and love our children. No other gift comes close to unconditional love; no amount of money, toys, trips to Disney World, nothing.

A biblical pattern for this relationship is that of David, royal leader of ancient Israel, and his rebellious third son Absalom (see 2 Samuel 13–19). Absalom had turned the people of the land against his father. He coveted David's position as king. Yet when word reached David that his ungrateful son had been killed in battle, David responded as a loving father, not as the mighty king of Israel. He retired to his chamber and wept. "O my son Absalom, my son, my son Absalom! Would I had died instead of you, O Absalom, my son, my son!" (2 Sam. 18:33b). Even three thousand years after it was uttered, we can feel the pathos and grief in that lament. Few youth in history have rebelled in such a dramatic and destructive way. Yet Papa David kept open the door of his heart, wishing he could have died in Absalom's place.

It raises the question of how we twentieth-century parents respond when parenting is painful, when we're disappointed and disillusioned, when we feel rejected or are the recipients of their full anger. When it comes from those as close as flesh and blood, it is grievous indeed. We can act as though we don't care. But who are we fooling? It hurts! David's heart must have been crushed. But with God's help he kept open his mind and heart and found the strength to forgive. He never ceased loving Absalom. David was a faithful parent to the very end.

Forgiveness has the wondrous power to set family members free to live together in peace and harmony. Without a forgiving attitude, bitterness of soul quickly takes over. Possibilities for emotional and spiritual growth are thwarted. Unforgiving attitudes can make life a burden not a blessing. I should know. Years ago I held a grudge against a person in the small community where we lived. It was just a misunderstanding, perhaps the result of a minor personality clash. The further it went, the worse it got. We went to great lengths to avoid each other. If I saw her car coming down the street, I turned at the first available corner and sped away. It got so I was on constant alert for autos like hers and for people who from a distance slightly resembled her. I'm not proud of how I behaved. Though my head knew the solution, I obviously lacked the will to act upon it. I stored up resentment for months and months. Believe me, a small amount of ill will can turn into mountains of suspicion. I might as well have been behind bars. Without intending for it to happen, my unforgiving feelings toward one person began to affect negatively my relationships with everybody else, including family.

Forgiveness frees people to love. It releases warm, positive feelings within our souls. Tons of effort and self-discipline aren't required because forgiveness cannot be forced. It's a gift of God through Christ and it issues from faithful, thankful hearts. Forgiving a person who may have wronged us, including a teen, does not mean we look the other way, that we ignore the issues or condone inappropriate behavior. Quite the opposite. True forgiveness looks the problem squarely in the eye and deals with it firmly and fairly.

At no time in the process does forgiveness reject the individual. It is forever accepting of others. When forgiveness is offered and received, it opens the way for reconciliation. It gives persons room to grow and freedom to change. It even allows the offending party to make additional mistakes and say other hurtful things without the slightest hint of trying to retaliate. Forgiveness isn't about control. It's about openness, about removing the barriers and obstacles that separate us from others, that can come between parents and youth. Forgiveness has the power to hold families together, to restore their fellowship and sense of community. It contains remarkable healing properties.

Show me a family who is active, who work and play and travel together, and I'll show you a family with conflicts and tensions. It's normal and necessitates the presence of forgiveness and its sidekick, forgetting. Of all people on earth, parents of teenagers need to practice the art of forgetfulness. No, I don't mean losing track of your car keys or where you put your wallet. We're talking about a godlike quality: the capacity to actively forget the unkind words, the slights and hurts that have entered your life.

The prophet Isaiah heard and reported this promise from God. "I will not remember your sins" (Isa. 43:25*b*). Thank goodness! If God kept a record of our shortcomings and the errors of our ways, we would be continually looking over our shoulders, expecting a lightning bolt to strike us. But the Eternal Parent is infinitely compassionate with us. We earthly parents are called to do the same with our children, who are every bit as human as we are. We are to release the hurts and pains, and our memories of them as well, and give youth a clean slate. If God must choose "not to remember" our sins, then we also must decide to forget our children's transgressions.

One secret of accomplishing this is tucked away in the words of the apostle Paul to the church at Corinth. He advises them as followers of Christ to "regard no one from a human point of view" (2 Cor. 5:16a). This is particularly important when your daughter or son is behaving in an exceedingly human manner. When a teen is camped out in the bathroom and you don't know how much longer you can wait; when he's slurping his cereal and it's 6:30 A.M. and you're still half-asleep; when she fails to let you know her whereabouts and it's a dark rainy night—those are the times when you really need to think of them from a divine point of view. You will still need to have a serious discussion about the problem, but your perspective will be transformed. You'll see their potential for learning, their possibilities for growth, and the beauty and goodness that are inside their souls. You'll still be upset and you have every right to be. But you'll react positively and creatively, with forgiveness and with great hopes for their future.

One effective way of keeping open the door of your heart is through the use of humor; good, clean humor of course. Complain, moan, and groan and your youth will likely turn a deaf ear. Smile and laugh and he or she will laugh with you, and in the process hear your message. Being a family is hard work. It's tough these days to be raising teenagers. Take the business of being a family seriously. But when you look at yourself in a mirror, a few chuckles are in order. There are ample reasons for happiness and laughter.

A sense of humor can defuse problems and tensions before they ever get started. It can assuage even grief. Just days before my father died, he bent me down to his bedside and whispered, "I want you to tell a joke at my memorial service."

"Pop," I protested, "that's supposed to be a somber and serious occasion. I can't tell a joke."

"At my service you can." He squeezed my hand hard. "Promise me you will." Against my better judgment I did, whereupon he told the story he wanted used, something about two men playing golf when a funeral procession went by. I can't remember the rest of it, let alone the punch line. But so what? The particular joke doesn't matter. It was his marvelously upbeat attitude toward life and death that was important. Yes, I told the joke, not nearly as well as he did, though I did get a smattering of laughs.

I do care about your family, including you as a parent. I'm truly saddened when I hear of trouble in a home anywhere on this earth. If that should occur to you, continue listening, forgiving, and caring. And don't rationalize or make excuses. Just get out there and love those teenagers with all your might. No matter what happens, keep open the door of your heart! Sooner or later, you and your family will be blessed.

16.
To Have Children or to Be a Family

*H*ere came our family parade, Mom and Pop followed by a lively group of stair-step children. I understand why people often stopped to ask, "How many do you have?" I could see them trying to count the continuously moving herd of youngsters.

"Six," we'd reply, sometimes adding, "at least the last time we looked." We'd receive looks of admiration or of compassion, and in today's overpopulated world, an occasional gently disapproving frown. I'd have the urge to explain to these latter folks that "Only three are homegrown. The others are store-bought." I usually held my tongue, but once in a while the old armchair philosopher in me would pop out. I had a standing order from their mom, my spouse, to keep it under wraps—especially when talking to strangers. But sometimes it simply wouldn't obey. "I'm sorry," I'd reply to their question. "We don't *have* any children. We *are* a family who happens to number six youngsters and two adults, plus a couple of dogs, a cat, and several other furry critters." I'm certain my distinction over verb usage completely escaped most inquirers, or at best mildly amused them.

For me, however, it was and is a substantive issue. It's important which verb you conjugate when referring to your family, either "to have" or "to be," because words indicate what is going on inside a person's head. Language is a direct expression of attitudes, beliefs, and values. And in our present-day Western culture, we talk a great deal about having; about buying, owning, and possessing, not only when it comes to material objects but also to ideas and people. "I have an idea," we frequently say, going on to tell what it is. Or we explain, "It's my belief that thus and such is true," as though beliefs belong to us, as if they're property that we own. They aren't. Thoughts and ideas and beliefs exist apart from our acceptance of them. Along with beauty, joy, and love, they have objective reality and will endure until the end of time.

The same is true of children and youth. They're individuals, unique and special; their very own persons. Parents give them their initial thrust into the world, but even when they're totally dependent creatures, they are not their parents' property. A baby is not a doll but a small person with needs and wants and feelings. Parents and other family members are responsible for their care and keeping, but God does not grant an exclusive franchise on their lives. Children are a gift from the Creator of life. Period. Therefore, when referring to people we really ought not use verbs that convey a sense of ownership. I do not *have* a son named John. Rather, John and I *are* father and son.

How we perceive others makes a major difference in the way we treat them. If I think you belong to me, I may act as though you're just another piece of furniture. You become an inanimate object I can move wherever I want, whenever I choose, and without ever consulting you. It doesn't matter what a couch or a table thinks. If I treat you as a thing, I will cherish you or discard you depending upon my moods and whims.

This possessive way of thinking about children and other persons is prevalent in our society. Listen to the question directed to the father of the bride in a traditional marriage ceremony. "Who gives this woman to be married to this man?" No human being can give, sell, barter, or trade another human life. That's a subtle form of slavery even when a family practices it with tender care and affection. Parents are stewards of their off-spring—caretakers and custodians, not possessors.

It's a significant differentiation. Parents who "have" children will deal with them the way an accountant adds and subtracts long lines of figures, calculating the expenses rather than delighting in the rich blessings. Admittedly, this next example is extreme. But it's a true story.

I was a friend of the two boys. Their father was a strict man, inflexible and unyielding. I never liked visiting their house when he was home. He made me nervous. He had a ledger, a thick, hardbound edition with lines and columns written in green ink in which he kept track of every penny he'd ever spent on these two lads. I mean every penny: groceries, school clothes, toothbrushes, each tube of toothpaste; their share of tissue and toilet paper, their portion of electricity, water, and garbage collection, all figured at 25 percent of the total; every pair of shoes they'd ever worn including an amount for new shoelaces. I am not making this up. It was all there in neat, tidy numbers, complete with weekly, monthly, and annual totals. And I'll bet if anybody had asked, their dad could have quickly calculated the grand total for their lives to that moment.

I can't imagine how much time it took to keep such detailed financial records. That alone would have been reason not to do it. Even as a youth, it seemed far more tragic to me than a mere waste of time. He had turned my two buddies into pencil marks in a musty book, into dollar and cent signs and decimal points. I always wanted to make off with that volume and drop it from a bridge into the river. I've never since heard of a parent who behaved in such a mean-spirited, miserly manner about family expenses. And I hope I never do.

I must confess, however, I've stored up mental records of how much extra hot water a teenager used for one shower; or how much unused milk was left in a cereal bowl; or how much heat they let out the front door by failing to close it tightly. Yes, youth need to learn responsibility. They must be taught the value of money. But as a parent, I do not need to keep a running account of what it's costing me. It's probably better not to know. If I behave in a stingy way, it's an indication I'm operating as though I "have" a family and that I apparently consider my investment in them to be a losing proposition. By the way, I never did find out if my friends' father presented them with a bill after they were out on their own.

When we "have" young persons in our family, the tendency is to try to buy their allegiance and pay for their obedience. It's easier, I suppose, to offer them an allowance than to make allowances for them; that is, to give them things rather than time, to offer money rather than love. True, material possessions don't talk back, pout, or argue. But they also cannot smile at you, give hugs, hold hands, or plant a kiss on your shiny forehead.

In the "having a family" mode, parents often become manipulative and controlling. Desired behavior is literally purchased with the promise of expensive presents. Youth in such systems should not think of these items as gifts. They are anything but. They come with an exceedingly high price tag: the loss of personal freedom and dignity. In the mode of "being a family," there are no strings attached to offers or requests, no secret conditions, no hidden agendas or fine print. The motivation for good deeds must grow within young persons themselves, pointing them toward lives of self-discipline and inner direction. This style of parenting recognizes that love is not a thing to be handed to teens but a process to be shared and lived with them.

When you "have" a family, stability and security are based on what you own or possess, things such as salaries, bank accounts, three-car garages, television sets and other electronic gadgets, closets stuffed with clothes, half of which will never be worn. Apparently it's reassuring to have them hanging there just in case. When we "are" a family, stability arises from our commitment to one another, from trust and confidence in one another's reliability, from knowing that integrity and faithfulness are part of all family relationships. In other words, it's a security that grows out of the deep, nurturing soil of love.

Parents who "have" authority in the family must work hard to keep it. Since it's an outward and visible characteristic, it's always in danger of being taken away or of getting lost. That type of parental power is grounded on factors such as who's physically the biggest and strongest, who's got the most money, or who's holding the remote control device in their hand. Maintaining this kind of authority is tiring. It can quickly wear out a parental body.

The better way is to "be" an authority with your family. This doesn't mean you have control over them. Yours is an inner power that bubbles up naturally from genuine concern and caring. It comes from giving without measure, from offering yourself wholly and without reservation. The first method, "having," almost guarantees that young people will be rebellious. The second approach to authority, "being," can make rebellion almost obsolete.

Some of the tensions we experience in family life today may result from how territorially we act. When we have and own things, we naturally seek to protect them. We become very aware of what is our space and what is their space. And woe be to others if they step uninvited into my territory. I'll label you a trespasser and figure out a way to prosecute. In the "have a family" mentality, members are very conscious of boundaries, focusing on the things that separate them from one another. And because age is one of those dividing lines, it's always crystal clear who is the parent and who is the teen, and that never shall the twain meet. The family becomes a collection of individuals who must protect their own space and defend their own rights. It becomes an "us against them" battle. Real peace is seldom possible under these conditions. The best you can hope for is a long-lasting truce.

When families are able to go with the flow, relax and just "be," the need to defend individual space is substantially lessened. People aren't jealous of what others receive or of the talents they enjoy. There is respect for one another that renders boundaries meaningless. Who needs walls and fences when people completely trust one another? It also means that parents don't have to go around acting like the police all the time. They can "let their hair down," reveal their childlikeness, and show their vulnerability; in a nutshell, they can be human. That makes them approachable and lovable. Parents and teens really aren't from two different planets. They're cut from the same cloth; poured out of the same mold. One is older and more experienced. The other is obviously younger and hasn't had as many opportunities to learn. But both are children of God and equally loved. When viewed from the perspective of eternity, the few years of chronological difference between parents and teens are but as an eye blink, a snap of the fingers.

"Being" a family permits trust to grow and freedom to flourish. I remember as a teenager that the more responsibly I behaved, the more freedom I was given. It wasn't always immediately and automatically given to me. Each step of the way I had to demonstrate I deserved it. However, I didn't constantly have to demand or fight for my rights. They were freely bestowed upon me at the appropriate time.

I appreciated my parents' wisdom in knowing where to take a stand with me and where not to. They seemed to comprehend the difference between passing fads and abiding values. For example, they put up with my interesting, nontraditional appearance, recognizing that the person inside those strange clothes was of infinite value, whereas the apparel would soon be out of style and gone. They never said a word when I wore blue suede shoes with pink laces; when I bought a red and black striped sweater to go with my fluorescent green pants, the ones with the legs pegged so much I had to take off my socks to put them on. They let me have a Princeton hairstyle, a flattop with long sides, which I greased heavily to form a ducktail in the back. I was something to behold, at least in the late 1950s.

What could I say when our teens decided to go with the grunge look, or a daughter borrowed a huge flannel shirt of mine? A son came home from high school one afternoon with a bemused look. "Guess what happened?" he said. "In Family Living class today the teacher asked a question. 'What would your parents say if you came to dinner with spiked purple hair?' " Most of his classmates reported that their parents would yell at them, demand that they wash the color out immediately, and/or burst into uncontrollable sobs.

"When it was your turn," I asked, "what did you say?"

"I said my folks would probably get the giggles and ask me if I needed new clothes to go with my fancy new 'do.'" His response pleased me. He knew that our love for him had little to do with his outward appearance. As long as he was clean, properly covered, and healthy, we'd be content. I do admit he made a strikingly handsome young man when he was decked out in his orchestra tuxedo. But styles change; fads come and go; and a teenager's inner person will be around for eternity. Parent them accordingly. End of sermon.

17.
Keep Them Busy and Other Questionable Advice

Advice for parents of teenagers is readily available and intended to be of help. But let the recipient beware. It isn't always of much value and actually can be of harm. Sort it through carefully and don't practice it just because somebody else preached it, even when it's hoary with age. What worked for another parent's teen may not be applicable to yours at all. It may have failed miserably with theirs and they just conveniently neglected to tell you. Graciously accept their suggestion, then give it your most rigorous possible test: apply common sense. When reviewing the merits of various advice, constantly keep a mental image of your daughter or son before you. Then remember how much you paid for that advice before you try it out in real life.

You've surely heard this theme multiple times. "A busy kid is a good kid." Or maybe your version is, "Idle hands are the devil's workshop." The theory is valid. If a person of any age is actively involved in positive things, there's less chance they will fritter time away. There will be fewer hours available for getting into mischief. The concept is particularly true with teenagers. Most of them aren't looking for trouble, but at their age it seems to find them quite readily. Wholesome, creative activities are highly recommended. As a bonus, it will probably cut down on the hours their eyeballs are glued to the television set.

Don't thoughtlessly and uncritically embrace this old adage, or any other for that matter. Like most good things, it can be overdone. The first thing to consider is your own motive as a parent. Why is it you want your youth actively participating in programs, groups, sports, and music? The correct answer is obvious: because it's good for them. Activities can be healthy for them physically, will help them build a strong self-image, and should enhance their people skills. Like anybody else, parents may have mixed motives. Did you sign them up for the debate team simply to get them out of the house and to give their jaw and mouth a good workout? Did you get them to join the soccer team or the drama department so you could receive a little praise and recognition for yourself? I have sat through too many youth baseball games not to know that parents' motives aren't always pure and lovely.

If you subscribe to the wise saying that active young people are happy young people, then recognize that the same advice is almost certainly true for you as well. This may be a radical suggestion, but parents should consider practicing what they preach. Get involved with your teen. You can't go out on the tennis court when they're in the middle of a match. But you can volunteer to practice with them, to help them with their forehand or serve. You don't have to be an accomplished player, just a willing one. A sense of humor will certainly help, too.

Parents are to be directors of youth activities, not promoters of mere busyness. You want to help them accomplish their own goals, not to push them into programs in which they have little interest. Look for skid marks. If the heels of their shoes scuff the floor as you push and pull them out the door, that's probably an indication they would rather not participate. When they were small children, you may have insisted anyway. But now they are too big to push somewhere they don't want to go. In addition, youth are developing a clearer concept of who they are, of what gifts and graces they have, and are capable of making most of their own decisions. In fact, you need to encourage them to make as many decisions as possible.

Another piece of sage advice says, "You learn by doing." In other words, supply teens with plenty of hands-on experience. Be wise and know when to serve as their guide and counselor, and when to function as a parental authority figure. You'll be the former more often than the latter as they increasingly mature. The basic parental goal is to be their lifetime friend. Remember this. It will help you to be thoughtful and gracious to them all along the way.

Sometimes youth need parents to "give them a brake," that is, to help them slow down a bit, to help them conserve energy when they're running on low. Youth are like the rest of us and can easily become overcommitted and stretched too thinly. You will bless them forever if you teach them to say "No!" when that's what's needed. They will learn that they cannot do everything and to concentrate their efforts on successfully completing a smaller number of projects. There are numerous adults who obviously have never learned this important lesson.

Even the Almighty took a day off to rest from the strenuous activity of creating. God worked hard for six days, then rested on the seventh in order to appreciate the beauty of his efforts and maybe to prepare for what he knew was coming. After all, he'd just turned the entire place over to humans. Yes, he gave them an instruction manual. No, they didn't pay much attention to it. Like all humans since that moment, they probably used it only as a last resort. On that first Sabbath, God may have wiped his brow and said, "Whew!" Then it was time to prepare for the eighth day onward.

We assume that keeping youth busy is mostly a matter of keeping them on the go and that it primarily means physical activity. Not so. Like their parents, youth need a balanced life with strenuous work and play followed by quiet times of thinking, meditating, reflecting, and resting. Our youngest son was quite active. He pedaled his bicycle all over town, had a paper route, and played on a baseball team for a while. But I shall always fondly remember him doing a mental activity: reading. He'd stay up considerably later than we thought he should, burrow under a thick stack of bedcovers, and by using a flashlight, finish reading his book.

I favor balancing a teen's outward activities between those involving team play and those of an individual or personal nature. Once they leave the formal academic setting, team sports become more difficult to organize. It's tough to find twenty-one other people and the equipment necessary to play a game of tackle football. But find one other willing soul and you can enjoy Ping-Pong, tennis, golf, bowling, and a host of other great activities. Walking, hiking, fishing, and bicycling can be done solo.

Then there's music. As a wee lad, I learned to play the violin. I couldn't take piano lessons because my sister was already doing so, and she was so accomplished that I had to find an instrument as different from hers as possible. Hence the violin. Okay, I screeched and scratched a lot at the beginning. But after a goodly number of lessons, I improved considerably. That was fortunate because my parents had to drive seventy miles one way across a mountain pass every Saturday morning. When I was in high school, I quit playing the fiddle for several important reasons: I was too busy with girls, sports, earning money, other girls, and wanting my peers to accept me. Playing a violin didn't seem like a very masculine thing to do when I was sixteen. I now practice only once or twice a year. I guess I'm still too busy. Well, I could turn off the television set.

The other day I heard someone ask my mother if she regretted all the time, effort, and money they'd invested in my music lessons. I figured it was none of that person's business, but she asked anyway. My mother's answer made me feel warm all over.

"Not at all," she replied. "Some day he'll probably have the time to practice again. And more valuable than actually playing music, he learned to appreciate it. I happen to know he loves music of all kinds." She's right, with the exception of rap and hard rock. When parents encourage and support their youth's involvement, they should go for long-term benefits, which are far more important than immediate results. The particular skills young people learn may or may not be useful later in their lives. But the commitment they must make and the discipline they have to demonstrate will hold them in good stead for the rest of their lives. It would indeed be nice to play the violin better, but I wouldn't exchange it for the love of music I gained. I'll just have to be content listening to Itzhak Perlman. The joy of music blesses me every day, year in, year out. My mother has reason not to be disappointed in me. Even though I didn't become a concert violinist, my parents invested wisely in those lessons.

Our primary responsibility as parents of teens is to help them discover what God has in store for them. Who were they created to be? What gifts did God give them and how should they effectively use them? These are tough questions with even tougher answers. Parents are not expected to beat the bushes to find specific employment for their young people. We aren't supposed to tell them what's best for them. They must find that out for themselves. The parental role is to enable them to find who they truly are, then assist them in matching their abilities and strengths to their chosen field or profession.

The goal for parents is not to get teens from age thirteen to age twenty as quickly and painlessly as possible. It is rather to cherish the relationships we have with them, to enjoy those years because there will never again be times and opportunities quite like them. Every so often, both teens and parents should take a giant step back from the struggle and savor the moment. It is a special time!

Youth have a ministry from God to fulfill that no other age group can do. Centuries upon centuries ago the prophet Joel explained that it is young people who will see visions. They have the God-given ability to look ahead, to see the world as it could and should be, and to envision the possibilities of the future. Along with their participation in sports, music, social events, clubs, church youth groups and the like, youth need to be reminded of their deeper purposes, of their responsibilities before God. Though the teen years are transitional, they still are of great significance. Teens have a service to render to society that they alone can give. Therefore, you parents out there, don't keep them too busy with minor details so that fulfilling their true mission gets crowded out.

There are other tidbits of advice that seem suspect to me, or at least subject to closer scrutiny. Take the oft-quoted phrase, "Give them an inch and they'll take a mile." First of all, that needs to be updated to read centimeters and kilometers. Second, it simply doesn't coincide with the majority of my experiences with youth. They frequently push the limits parents set for them but not to that extreme. It implies a constant battle between the generations that isn't there or certainly doesn't have to be.

Parents and teens are not adversaries. They're members of the same family, compatriots in the search for meaning and purpose in life, spiritual sisters and brothers. Parents and youth should negotiate their differences and meet halfway. If my math is correct, that would bring them together at 2,640 feet down the path. Whatever the exact measurement, you get the point. Rather than glaring at one another from across the distance between an inch and a mile, compromise and start walking. Meet at the middle and enjoy one another's company.

Or how about the admonition that parents should never disagree in front of the kids? Yes, parents should avoid major blowups and angry arguments, but those aren't desirable whether the kids are around or not. It's my opinion that clearing the air on occasion is healthy for families, at least when it's done with caring and kindness. Honesty among people is always a plus. And who do parents think they're fooling? The kids' antennae are constantly out to receive signals from their parents. They know what's really going on and how Dad and Mom are feeling about each other. It helps teens see that normal relationships have stresses and conflicts, but with love and understanding those can all be resolved. When they relate to each other openly and truthfully, parents can model the way of forgiving love. They can demonstrate the reality and power of reconciliation. It will provide young persons with a more realistic concept of adult family relationships.

I don't have any idea how many times I've heard someone say, "There's no use crying over spilt milk." That's literally true. It's better to get a mop or paper towels and just start cleaning up the mess. However, it's usually spoken in a figurative way, implying that we shouldn't show emotion when something goes wrong. You've got to be strong and silent and hold it all inside. Wrong! I say get those frustrations out where you can creatively deal with them. You don't have to dump them on somebody else. Go dig in the garden. Hammer a few nails into hardwood. Take the dog for a brisk walk. Clean the garage. Cry. These are far more healing than bottling up your emotions. It's easier for others around you than if you fuss and fume, or cuss and swear. It's okay to have and express feelings in a family, even when the kids are watching. Do you have any idea how hard it is to get close to someone who seems perfect, who never admits to being lonely or sad, who makes the ancient Stoics seem like wimps? Real parents will receive real love from real youth. That's what being family is all about.

I wish a store somewhere would sell a plaque or sign that reads, "Welcome, Family at Work. Maturity Under Construction. Enter at Your Own Risk." I'd permanently place it by our front door to indicate that things are happening inside our house and inside our souls. People are growing. Things are changing. Trust is being built. And love abounds. Hallelujah!

18.
The Teen Commandments for Parents

1. In parenting teens, thou shalt have far more "Thou shalts" than "Shalt nots."

2. Whenever possible, thou shalt draw energy from teens rather than be drained by them. Be of good cheer. They have plenty of vitality and enthusiasm to go around.

3. Thou shalt make allowances for them as well as give allowances to them.

4. Honor thyself as a parent. Do not shoulder all the blame when they make mistakes and do not take all the credit when they succeed.

5. Thou shalt go the second mile with your teen. Then thou shalt go the third mile, the fourth, or however far it takes. Try thy best to take every step of the journey with joy.

6. Thou shalt listen to young people as much as or more than thou shalt talk to them.

7. Thou shalt never so much as touch a teen's diary or journal. Thou shalt not pry. Enjoy what they choose to reveal of themselves and trust what you do not yet know. In all things, respect their privacy.

8. Thou shalt remember thine own soul's needs, getting away from the pressures of parenting from time to time in order to renew your commitment to the task.

9. Children and youth do not belong to you. They are not possessions but persons, gifts from God who are temporarily entrusted into your care. Therefore, thou shalt not *have* children; thou shalt *be* a family.

10. Thou shalt assist teens in discovering the plans and joys God has in store for them, helping them use their unique abilities and talents for the glory of God.